SIGHT AND SENSIBILITY

Sight and Sensibility

Evaluating Pictures

DOMINIC MCIVER LOPES

CLARENDON PRESS · OXFORD

OXFORD

UNIVERSITY PRESS

Great Clarendon Street, Oxford OX2 6DP

Oxford University Press is a department of the University of Oxford.
It furthers the University's objective of excellence in research, scholarship,
and education by publishing worldwide in

Oxford New York

Auckland Cape Town Dar es Salaam Hong Kong Karachi
Kuala Lumpur Madrid Melbourne Mexico City Nairobi
New Delhi Shanghai Taipei Toronto

With offices in

Argentina Austria Brazil Chile Czech Republic France Greece
Guatemala Hungary Italy Japan Poland Portugal Singapore
South Korea Switzerland Thailand Turkey Ukraine Vietnam

Oxford is a registered trade mark of Oxford University Press
in the UK and in certain other countries

Published in the United States
by Oxford University Press Inc., New York

© Dominic Lopes 2005

The moral rights of the author have been asserted
Database right Oxford University Press (maker)

First published 2005

British Library Cataloguing in Publication Data

Data available

Library of Congress Cataloging in Publication Data

Data available

Typeset by Newgen Imaging Systems (P) Ltd., Chennai, India
Printed in Great Britain
on acid-free paper by
Biddles Ltd,
King's Lynn, Norfolk

ISBN 0-19-927734-6   978-0-19-927734-6

1 3 5 7 9 10 8 6 4 2

For Susan Herrington

PREFACE

There's more to the picture than meets the eye.
Hey hey, my my.

Neil Young

Search Google Images for 'philosophy' and you will find yourself a few clicks away from almost 200,000 images allegedly having something to do with philosophy. Search for 'pictures' and you will net 3,500,000 hits. Pictures, once a rare and precious good, have been easy and cheap to reproduce for 200 years, thanks to printing technologies. Photography and now digital imaging have made pictures as easy to make as to reproduce, and hence as commonplace as text. Should we view this change with gratitude or trepidation? It is hard to know even where to look for an answer (not Google!). What is clear is that we must guard against some deep and possibly irrational misgivings about pictures.

The art historian Barbara Stafford has documented how pictures are 'everywhere transmitted, universally viewed, but as a category generally despised. Spectatorship itself has become synonymous with empty gaping, not thought-provoking attention' (1996: 11). Some theorists put the point more provocatively, alleging that pictures are by nature pornographic. This means not that they are sexual in content but rather that they necessarily promote 'empty gaping'.

The trouble, for these theorists, is that pictures are visual. An influential and typical example is the opening sentence of Fredric Jameson's *Signatures of the Visible*: 'the visual is *essentially* pornographic, which is to say that it has its end in rapt, mindless fascination'. Focusing on moving pictures, Jameson goes on to conclude that 'pornographic films are thus the only potentiation of films in general, which ask us to stare at the world as though it were a naked body' (1990:1). Pictures are visual representations, and vision is 'pornographic', so pictures are *essentially* pornographic. The very medium of depiction thwarts serious thought, secures our acquiescence to oppressive social structures, and deprives us of the intellectual resources necessary to resist its propagandizing.

Many picture theorists also blame the aesthetic finish of pictures for covering up their underlying emptiness. Pictures have no redeeming value, and our attributions of aesthetic value to them license us to engage in empty gaping under the pretence of high culture. Curiously, we try to *define* pictorial art as non-pornographic, reasoning that if something is art, it cannot be pornography. Critics of pictures reply that at least smut is honest; everything else is smut in fancy dress.

This should not be dismissed as the usual academic claptrap, for the academics have touched upon a widespread anxiety about visual representation. Several cultures, past and present, have imposed prohibitions or taboos against images. Painters of the French Academy considered optical experience an inadequate basis for pictorial art, which they thought must tell stories or teach lessons. More locally, parents get anxious when their children look at comic books instead of reading 'real' books, and the perceived seriousness of a newspaper or magazine is proportional to the ratio of text to image in its pages. Stereotypes are called 'images', and it is *images* of this and that (women's bodies, black men's bodies, household appliances, perfect suburban lawns) that are said to shape how we think and what we want. Finally, when it comes to smut, it is pictures that we worry about, rarely text. Granted, we may appreciate the redemptive value of pictures as art, instruction, and entertainment. The lesson is that people are ambivalent about pictures.

For Jameson, nothing redeems pictures their faults, and any appearance to the contrary is a cover-up. He charges the scholar of pictures and vision with the task of exposing their pornographic heart.

If Jameson overstates his thesis, and the truth is that we are ambivalent about pictures, then scholars should diagnose and inoculate us against any tendency to put pictures down.

Many pictures are no good, but many deserve our highest appreciation. We need a conception of pictures that enables us to evaluate them on a case-by-case basis. Since pictures' critics diagnose them with a terminal visual disease, it is up to their defenders to explain how their visuality is sometimes a blessing and only sometimes a curse. The blessing, when it is aesthetic, must be real and not a placebo. *Sight and Sensibility* defends pictures along these lines.

The past two centuries have seen a revolution in imaging technologies, from lithography to the internet, that is doing for pictures what the print revolution did for writing. No wonder there is a great deal of public debate about their impact. Unfortunately, the debate is often skewed by a deep-seated and unexamined ambivalence about the visuality of pictures. The time has come for us to look into the evaluation of pictures as visual representations, for only then can we negotiate the challenges posed by an increasingly image-saturated, image-based culture.

Many individuals graciously gave their time to the improvement of the manuscript. Peter Goldie, Matthew Kieran, Stephanie Ross, James Shelley, Nan Stalnaker, and Chris Stephens read drafts of individual chapters or portions of them. Audiences at the University of North Carolina, the American Society for Aesthetics Pacific Division, Auburn University, the University of British Columbia, the Institut Jean Nicod, the University of Maribor, the University of Adelaide, and the University of Sydney posed challenges and made helpful suggestions. The manuscript was read in its entirety by Susan Herrington, Robert Hopkins, Derek Matravers, Bob Stecker, members of my 2003 seminar in aesthetics, and the Press's anonymous referees. I thank them all for their stamina and shrewd advice.

I also thank Bernadette Andrade and Ron Fong for their cheerful and efficient administrative support, which especially smoothed the chore of obtaining permission to reproduce the images that illustrate this volume.

Parts of Chapter 5 that discuss illustrations of Dante's *Inferno* began as a paper written for Allen Dunn and John McGowan's NEH Seminar on Literature and Value. That paper was published in 2000 in volume 83 of *Soundings*. Permission to use this material is gratefully acknowledged.

A Clowes Fellowship at the National Humanities Center gave this book its initial push, and I am indebted to the Center's staff for making my stay there productive and pleasant. I also acknowledge the Social Sciences and Humanities Research Council of Canada, the Peter Wall Institute for Advanced Studies, and the University of British Columbia for supplying time during which the remainder of the book was written.

Work on this book began about the time I joined the philosophy department at UBC. Writing a book is difficult, but I cannot imagine having written this one without the company of stimulating, open-minded, and also exacting colleagues and students. Among these, I am particularly grateful to Mohan Matthen and Catherine Wilson for their unstinting support, perceptive advice, and fine example.

DML

Vancouver, Canada
September 2004

CONTENTS

LIST OF ILLUSTRATIONS

INTRODUCTION

If you buy a painting you also buy the look of the thing it represents.

John Berger

Mounted upon the wall behind the woman in Vermeer's *Woman Holding a Balance* is another painting, one whose subject is the Last Judgement (Fig. 1). The theme of judgement is repeated in the balance which the woman uses to weigh her goods. By juxtaposing moral and commercial evaluation, Vermeer draws our thoughts to evaluation in general and so to the evaluation of pictures in particular. Pictures are worth owning, some more than others. They sometimes make good decorations, adorning palaces, dentists' offices, and counting-houses. Some are displayed in public or private as badges of social status or group membership. Some impart lessons, as does the painting depicted in *Woman Holding a Balance*, or supply evidence for historical and scientific hypotheses, such as the claim that painters of Vermeer's time used the camera obscura. Very often, pictures are also objects of aesthetic evaluation. This book concerns the aesthetic evaluation of pictures, viewed in relation to other evaluations of them.

You may find Degas's *Woman with Field Glasses* in Figure 2 somewhat offputting. Originally made as a sketch for part of a painting of a scene at the races, the drawing depicts a young woman looking through a pair of binoculars as if directly at you, the viewer. What might disarm you is not merely that she seems to look at you, but that she seems to look *back* at you—indeed, to scrutinize you exactly as closely and as freely as you scrutinize her, or the drawing of her. In fact, she is not looking at you: the drawing is a marked surface that depicts a woman looking through binoculars, but she never

Fig. 1. Johannes Vermeer, *Woman Holding a Balance*, 1664. Image © 2004 Board of Trustees, National Gallery of Art, Washington.

looked at you, and the drawing does not depict her as looking at you. Still, what it does depict—a woman looking straight out through binoculars—draws your attention to your act of looking at the picture and at her. *Woman with Field Glasses* is about our visual encounter with pictures and the scenes they depict. That is a second concern of this book.

Fig. 2. Edgar Degas, *Woman with Field Glasses*, 1865. Photo credit: HIP/Scala/Art Resource, NY.

Neither concern is new. Philosophers have long debated aesthetic value and evaluation, on the one hand, and experiences of pictures and depicted scenes on the other (e.g. Beardsley 1981; Dickie 1988; Goldman 1995*a*; Sibley 2001*a*; Schier 1986; Walton 1990; Lopes 1996; Hopkins 1998; Wollheim 1998; Kulvicki 2003). Moreover, what has been said about aesthetic value and evaluation applies to pictures as much as it applies to music, poetry, or landscape. All the same, the role of experiences of pictures and depicted scenes in the evaluation of pictures is, with few exceptions, scarcely given serious thought (the exceptions are Schier 1993; Graham 1994; Goldman 1995*b*; Hopkins 1997).

Bridging both concerns is an assumption about what it is to evaluate a picture as a picture:

pictorial evaluation thesis: *in part*, to evaluate a picture as a picture is to evaluate it as eliciting experiences of the picture itself and as of the scene it depicts.

No account of evaluating a picture *as a picture* will be complete if it ignores the part played by experiences of the picture and the scene it depicts. This thesis invites us to see what we can learn about our experiences of pictures and the scenes they depict from the evaluation of them, and what we can learn about the evaluation of pictures from our experiences of them and the scenes they depict. It invites us to deliberate upon sight and sensibility together.

The pictorial evaluation thesis is a starting-point, not a conclusion, though the more we learn by assuming its truth, the more reason we have to believe it. Two ambitions that overarch *Sight and Sensibility* spring from and unpack the pictorial evaluation thesis. The first is to defend a view about how aesthetic and non-aesthetic evaluations of pictures interact.

A Plea for Aesthetics

Those who doubt that anything sensible can be said about aesthetic evaluation usually have in mind narrow theories of the aesthetic. Art scholars outside philosophy tend to equate theories of aesthetic evaluation with a Kantian aesthetics, which they reject as narrow, and with it the whole enterprise of aesthetics (e.g. Smith 1988). A good response is to argue that aesthetic and non-aesthetic evaluations of pictures form an interactive web.

Woman Holding a Balance brings home that pictures can be the targets of many kinds of evaluation—commercial, social, cognitive, and aesthetic, to name a few. This is hardly news, but one may wonder whether there are any interesting logical connections between different kinds of evaluations of pictures. According to

aesthetic interactionism: aesthetic evaluations of pictures, while distinct from cognitive and moral evaluations, sometimes imply or are sometimes implied by non-aesthetic evaluations of those pictures.

Call this view 'interactionism' for short (the name is borrowed from Stecker 2005). The view is correct if some moral or political evaluations of pictures, for instance, imply aesthetic evaluations of those pictures, or if some aesthetic evaluations of pictures imply epistemic or cognitive evaluations of them.

Interactionism is widely spurned, for several reasons. To begin with, it requires that there be a genuine or distinct kind of aesthetic evaluation. Suppose, for example, that moral evaluations are really aesthetic evaluations in disguise. Then any moral evaluation will imply an aesthetic one if it implies another moral evaluation. Switching from a caricature of Nietzsche to a caricature of Bourdieu, suppose that aesthetic evaluations are really evaluations of social status. Then aesthetic evaluations imply social evaluations if they imply any other social evaluations.

The lesson is that interactionism is informative and interesting only in so far as it predicts logical concourse between distinct kinds of evaluation. Moreover, to sound a methodological note, showing that interactionism is true requires an independent idea of which evaluations are aesthetic and which are not. In the absence of such an idea, opponents of interactionism are free to insist that any case in which an aesthetic evaluation is alleged to imply or follow from a non-aesthetic evaluation in fact concerns two aesthetic evaluations or two non-aesthetic evaluations.

Chapter 3 sets forth a rule which distinguishes aesthetic evaluations from non-aesthetic ones. Since an evaluation is simply a representation of some object or some kind of object as having a merit or demerit, aesthetic evaluations represent objects or kinds of objects as having aesthetic merits or demerits. Traditional theories of aesthetic evaluation specify which merits or demerits are aesthetic—familiar candidates include beauty and ugliness, unity and disunity, and the tendency to engender or else interfere with a certain kind of experience. Chapter 3 eschews this strategy; it does not assume that aesthetic evaluations attribute specifically aesthetic merits and demerits. It allows, on the contrary, that typically non-aesthetic merits or demerits can be attributed in aesthetic evaluations; the rule it sets forth describes an aesthetic–non-aesthetic conversion mechanism. The rule is inherently friendly to but does not imply interactionism; anyone who embraces the former should, but need not, prefer the latter.

Interactionism contradicts the eliminativist view that aesthetic evaluations are not genuine because they are social evaluations or descriptions in disguise. No direct argument will be given against eliminativism. Instead, it will be assumed that aesthetic evaluation is a genuine, distinct type of evaluation, with the rule set forth in Chapter 3 specifying what precisely is being assumed.

Those attracted to eliminativism might nevertheless ponder two questions. Is the view taken in this book, that there are genuine aesthetic evaluations, more plausible once aesthetic evaluations are no longer construed as judgements of beauty, unity, significant aesthetic experience, or anything of the sort? And is a non-eliminativist view more plausible if aesthetic evaluations are not construed as autonomous but rather as interacting with other evaluations? The appeal of eliminativism flows from repulsion at identifying aesthetic merit with such items as beauty and at confining the aesthetic to a rarefied realm apart.

Interactionism is inconsistent with eliminativism and also aesthetic autonomism. In fact, there are many species of aesthetic autonomism and hence a corresponding variety of interactionisms. Aesthetic evaluations are autonomous with respect to type of non-aesthetic evaluation, V, if and only if no aesthetic evaluations imply or are implied by V-evaluations. Likewise, aesthetic evaluations interact with V-evaluations if and only if some aesthetic evaluations imply or are implied by V-evaluations.

For example, you may deny that aesthetic evaluations of pictures ever imply or are implied by moral evaluations, and yet may allow that aesthetic evaluations of pictures sometimes imply or are implied by cognitive evaluations. You are an autonomist with respect to moral evaluations and an interactionist with respect to cognitive evaluations. Commitment to one flavour of autonomism or interactionism does not imply commitment to any other. Interactionism, like autonomism, is henceforth to be construed as relative to one or another kind of non-aesthetic evaluation.

Several hypotheses can be stated with this point in mind. One is

aesthetic saturation: for any type of non-aesthetic evaluation, V, some aesthetic evaluations imply or are implied by some V-evaluation.

The hypothesis is that aesthetic evaluations can have logical concourse with evaluations of any other kind. No variety of autonomism is tenable. Equally ambitious is

aesthetic quarantine: for any type of non-aesthetic evaluation, V, no aesthetic evaluation implies or is implied by any V-evaluation.

In other words, no flavour of interactionism is tenable. Aesthetic evaluations may have logical concourse only with descriptions or with other aesthetic evaluations.

One argument for interactionism with respect to a given type of non-aesthetic evaluation, such as moral or cognitive evaluation, invokes aesthetic saturation. A parallel argument for autonomism with respect to moral or cognitive evaluation—or any other type of non-aesthetic evaluation—appeals to aesthetic quarantine. Some autonomists have invoked aesthetic quarantine, sometimes as a self-evident truth, and vestiges of this kind of aestheticism can be found in surprising corners of contemporary culture. Many people sometimes suggest that the aesthetic inhabits a realm apart from all other realms of value.

Aesthetic quarantine and saturation are implausible, and no respectable argument has been given for either. More plausible and defensible is

aesthetic articulation: there are some types of non-aesthetic evaluations, V, such that some aesthetic evaluations imply or are implied by some V-evaluations.

This view entails bare interactionism and is inconsistent with bare autonomism, but accommodates interactionism with respect to some kinds of non-aesthetic evaluation and autonomism with respect to others.

Anyone who accepts aesthetic articulation must take an interest in cataloguing and analysing varieties of non-aesthetic evaluation and how each relates to aesthetic evaluation. Indeed, the choice between interactionism and autonomism for any kind of non-aesthetic evaluation flows as a matter of course from such a catalogue and analysis.

Moreover, whether interactionism is interesting depends on what kinds of evaluations have logical relations with aesthetic evaluations. Nobody will be surprised to learn, for instance, that finding aesthetic merit in a picture implies, all things being equal, that the picture has some commercial worth. It is more difficult and instructive to find out whether moral evaluations of pictures imply aesthetic ones and, if so, *which* moral evaluations imply aesthetic ones. Close inspection is needed to discern how moral and aesthetic evaluations are related, if at all.

Chapter 4 argues that certain cognitive evaluations of pictures imply aesthetic evaluations, and Chapter 5 argues that some moral evaluations of pictures imply aesthetic evaluations. In each case the challenge is to identify which cognitive and moral evaluations imply aesthetic ones. We shall see that meeting the challenge means rethinking the nature of cognitive and moral evaluations of pictures.

The choice to study the cognitive and moral evaluation of pictures is not arbitrary. Interactionism with respect to the cognitive and moral evaluation of pictures is hotly disputed. More importantly, these disputes are not pointless: they go to the heart of what matters.

Autonomists may grant that pictures can be assessed for their contributions to thought, even moral thought, and still deny that these assessments can have any truck with aesthetic assessments. They insist that aesthetic evaluation should be strictly segregated in our reasoning about the value of pictures.

To dramatize the issue, consider what it takes to be a philistine. A philistine is not merely somebody with bad taste, who mistakes aesthetically bad for aesthetically good works or aesthetically good for aesthetically bad ones. Rather, the philistine issues mistaken aesthetic evaluations because his evaluations respond to the wrong kinds of considerations, such as a picture's popularity, or its match with his décor. By contrast, a person with bad taste who is not also a philistine makes aesthetic evaluations on the basis of what is aesthetically relevant, albeit with sorry results. Given this distinction between philistines and aesthetic unfortunates, we may ask whether a person is a philistine whenever he allows cognitive or moral evaluations to play a role in arriving at or justifying aesthetic evaluations.

Is Senator Helms a philistine for having condemned the photographs in Robert Mapplethorpe's X Portfolio, denying them any aesthetic merit by reason of what he took to be their immorality? Are some feminist art critics philistines when they elevate Judy Chicago's 'cunt art' simply for the moral and political ideals it embodies? Autonomists with respect to moral evaluations answer 'yes', whereas interactionists with respect to those evaluations reply 'no'. (Both may reject the moral verdicts of Mapplethorpe's detractors or Chicago's boosters. Whether one is a philistine is independent of the truth of one's moral views.)

Notice that the fissure between autonomists and interactionists transects the spectrum from left to right in civic and artworld politics. Some say that if great pictures have much aesthetic merit, and if having much aesthetic merit is incompatible with effective political advocacy, then a picture, in so far as it aspires to greatness, may have no truck with social and political advocacy. Backing this view are nineteenth-century aesthetes and twentieth-century formalists. Others, call them 'postmodernists', say that if aesthetic merit dwindles with attempts at political advocacy, then so much the worse for the claim that great depiction has to do with aesthetic merit—great pictures must be reconceived as political instead of aesthetic triumphs. The aesthetic prettifies and domesticates (and hence degrades) great painting. The postmodernists share with the aesthetes and formalists an autonomist presumption that aesthetic merit is incompatible with another value.

One source of anxiety about interactionism is the long dominance, at least in European culture, of moralism. Moralism takes several forms. According to one, aesthetic evaluations of pictures are overridden by moral evaluations. The aesthetic fineness of a picture is as nothing against its moral turpitude—indeed, aesthetic fineness can convert moral wrongness into gross moral corruption. According to another form of moralism, moral evaluations of pictures always imply *pro tanto* aesthetic evaluations of pictures. Moral condemnation always counts against a picture evaluated aesthetically, and moral praise always counts aesthetically in its favour.

A viable interactionism should explain why we are right to resist moralism by showing that moral and aesthetic evaluations only sometimes interact and at other times bypass each other entirely. Chapter 5 takes up this task.

A second source of anxiety about interactionism is an anxiety specifically about pictures. We are ambivalent about both the cognitive and the moral value of pictures. We are pulled in one direction by the likes of Picasso's potent critique of war in *Guernica* and the photographs of Dorothea Lange, which transformed popular conceptions of poverty during the Great Depression. Yet lurking in the background of much we say and think about pictures is the worry that they are not much good, cognitively or morally, in contrast with the other system of communication we frequently use, namely language.

A plausible conjecture is that our ambivalence about the cognitive and moral evaluation of pictures is due in part to their visuality. We hope to insulate pictures from any doubts about their cognitive or moral merit that stem from their visuality by isolating aesthetic from cognitive and moral evaluation.

This is one attraction of formalism, which quarantines aesthetic evaluation from moral and cognitive evaluation by restricting aesthetic evaluation to the formal, non-depictive elements of pictures while allowing cognitive and moral evaluations the free run of pictures' non-formal, depictive elements. The pictorial evaluation thesis directly contradicts the formalism of Clive Bell, whose slogan was that 'the representative element in a work of art may or may not be harmful; always it is irrelevant' (1913: 27). Chapter 3 gives an argument against formalism, but it is worth adding that formalism is a desperate strategy. We should wonder whether we use it simply to provide cover for what one might consider the nefarious work of pictures—so allege feminist critics writing about the male gaze in pictures, a topic taken up in Chapter 5. As an alternative to hiding behind formalism, let us take a hard look at whether the visuality of pictures is a proper source of concern.

Look Out

A second ambition of this book is to explain what it is for pictures to elicit experiences of the scenes they depict. This ambition arises from the pictorial evaluation thesis, which states that to evaluate a picture as a picture is in part to evaluate it as eliciting visual experiences of the picture itself and as of the scene it depicts. Put another way, the ambition is to develop a conception of the visuality of pictures which helps to explain what it is to evaluate pictures as visual.

As we have already seen, accepting the visuality of pictures may drive us into the arms of certain strains of autonomism. The reasoning is roughly this: in so far as they are visual, pictures have little cognitive or moral merit. So if we accept interactionism in respect of cognitive and moral evaluation, then pictures have little aesthetic merit as visual devices. Alternatively, some pictures have aesthetic merit as visual devices only if we reject interactionism in respect of cognitive and moral evaluation. 'Aesthetes' and formalists reject interactionism; critics of pictures (e.g. feminist critics of the gaze) deny that pictures have much cognitive, moral, or aesthetic merit.

Suppose that some pictures have aesthetic merit as visual devices and also that we endorse interactionism with respect to moral and cognitive evaluation. In that case we must show that pictures have cognitive and moral merit as visual representations. Showing this requires an adequate conception of the visuality of pictures.

Chapters 1 and 2 propose a conception of our experiences of pictures that grounds a defence of their value as visual representations. Developing such a conception is no trivial matter given certain assumptions. One is the

mimesis thesis: pictures typically elicit experiences as of the scenes they depict, which experiences resemble, in important respects, face-to-face experiences of the same scenes.

Woman Holding a Balance depicts a balance, and when you look at it, you typically have an experience as of a balance—you see a balance *in* the picture. *Woman with Field Glasses* depicts binoculars, and you typically see binoculars in it. According to the mimesis thesis, the experience of seeing the binoculars in the drawing is of a piece with the experience of seeing binoculars face to face. (It should not be read as invoking any of the many other uses of 'mimesis'.)

This is a robust conception of the visuality of pictures. Some will oppose it because it does not seem to them true to the character of our experience of pictures or because it seems inconsistent with our evaluations of pictures. They will ask how seeing an object in a picture can differ in value from an experience of seeing the object face to face. Surely seeing a common earthenware jug in a still-life painting by Chardin differs markedly in value from seeing a very similar earthenware jug in one's pantry? Chapter 1 reformulates these questions as 'The Puzzle of Mimesis' and answers them, not by rejecting the mimesis thesis but by giving it the right interpretation.

It is one thing to show that pictures can be evaluated as vehicles for seeing-in, but the pictorial evaluation thesis demands more than this. It says that to evaluate a picture *as a picture* is in part to evaluate it as a vehicle for seeing-in. Two claims form the backdrop of this assertion. One is that pictures are necessarily vehicles for seeing-in. The second is that to evaluate a picture as a picture is to evaluate it as the kind of thing it is. The two claims together explain why an evaluation of a picture as a picture is in part an evaluation of it as a vehicle for seeing-in.

The psychologist J. J. Gibson wrote that

the painter who is a decorator and the painter who is a depictor are different people and should not be confused. Aesthetics … has nothing to do with it. We can distinguish between a surface as an aesthetic object and a surface as a display of information. The surface that displays information may *also* be an aesthetic object, but the cases are different. A *picture* is a surface that always specifies something other than what it is. (1979: 273)

Gibson is right that a picture need not be an object of aesthetic evaluation, whereas it must be an object of perceptual interpretation (or processing). A distinction should be drawn between a surface as a display of a certain kind of information and a surface as an 'aesthetic object'. But drawing the distinction must not obscure the fact that a surface is a pictorial 'aesthetic object' only in so far as it displays information. Pictures need not be objects of aesthetic evaluation, but when they are objects of aesthetic evaluation *as pictures*, then they are objects of aesthetic evaluation *as information displays*.

Interactionism should be amended if it is to stand upon the pictorial evaluation and mimesis theses. In particular, it must take account of the visuality of pictures. According to

amended interactionism with respect to V: there are some types of non-aesthetic evaluation, V, such that some aesthetic evaluations of pictures as vehicles for seeing-in imply or are implied by some V-evaluations of pictures as vehicles for seeing-in.

This book examines how certain non-aesthetic evaluations of pictures may imply or be implied by aesthetic evaluations of pictures specifically *as vehicles for seeing-in.*

It is natural to focus on cognitive evaluation, because seeing-in is a kind of cognition. It is also permissible to ignore non-aesthetic evaluations that are not plausibly evaluations of pictures as vehicles for seeing-in. Commercial evaluations, to take an obvious example, may be ignored: aesthetic praise for a picture may imply that it has some commercial worth, but not that it has commercial worth as a vehicle for seeing-in. Not all interactions help develop a robust conception of the visuality of pictures.

Horizons

This book first outlines a robust conception of the visuality of pictures and then defends a model of how to evaluate pictures as visual. These aims are limited, however. An acknowledgement of the book's limitations cements any plausibility that might attach to its conclusions.

First, *Sight and Sensibility* concerns only representational pictures. This is a consequence of the mimesis thesis, which provides a rough-and-ready test of what counts as a representational picture—one that typically elicits experiences as of the scene it depicts (experiences of seeing-in) which importantly resemble face-to-face experiences of the same scene. We do not see Abraham, or even a human figure, in Barnett Newman's zip painting entitled *Abraham,* so the painting is not representational. The claim is not that Abraham is no part of the content of the experience you have when looking at *Abraham*—he might be, if the zip brings him to mind. All the same, he does not figure in your experience in the way he does when you see him face to face, and it is this that the mimesis thesis requires.

The mimesis thesis does not detail how Abraham figures in both seeing-in and face-to-face seeing. Is seeing-in *exactly like* face-to-face seeing? If not, then what should we say about the matter? Zip paintings aside, there is no denying that it is unclear how to draw a line between representational pictures and non-representational paintings. It is premature to clarify by stipulation: Chapter 1 details how seeing-in relates to seeing face to face and thus accounts for the visuality of pictures.

It would also be a mistake to construe the mimesis thesis too narrowly, however. Grant for now that pictures that are often called 'abstract' count as representational. Picasso's cubist pictures are sometimes called 'abstract', but they are representational because we see in them the scenes they depict—the experiences we have as of mandolins and winebottles resemble in the right ways face-to-face experiences of mandolins and winebottles. Suppose that in the case of non-representational or 'non-objective' paintings (like Newman's) but not in the case of merely abstract pictures (like Picasso's), we have no experiences of seeing-in at all like experiences of seeing face to face.

Could it be a mistake to set non-representational paintings aside? In fact, we might make one of two different mistakes.

Richard Wollheim has suggested that we see three-dimensional shapes and colours in the two-dimensional surfaces of Hans Hoffman paintings (1987: 62). If Wollheim is right, then the Newmans and Hoffmans are representational. So the first mistake might be to overlook some representational pictures.

This mistake, if it is a mistake, is benign. What is involved in evaluating the Newman or the Hoffman differs markedly from what is involved in evaluating the Vermeer and the Degas. The former pair embodies a conception of the proper aims and materials of painting removed by many decades and many rounds of cultural evolution from the latter pair. Still, what we will have learned about evaluating the Vermeer and the Degas *as vehicles for seeing-in* should apply also to the evaluation of Newmans and Hoffmans *as vehicles for seeing-in.* That Newmans and Hoffmans should be evaluated differently in other respects does not show that they should be evaluated differently as vehicles for seeing-in.

We make a different mistake if we do not see anything in the Newmans and Hoffmans (or if what we see in them is not relevant to their evaluation), and yet we do evaluate them as pictures. Here the mistake is to assume that to evaluate pictures as vehicles for seeing-in is even part of what is required to evaluate them as pictures. Some suggest that the history of painting in the twentieth century showed that mimesis is not essential to the medium of picturing. The charge would be that this book ignores an important history lesson.

This mistake, if it is one, is also harmless. The conclusions of this book may apply only to pictures that are representational. The claim that to evaluate a picture as a picture is to evaluate it as a vehicle for seeing-in is true provided that 'picture' means 'representational picture' or 'picture that sustains seeing its depictum in it'. This semantic stipulation does not impeach the tactic of setting aside non-representational pictures; rather, it vindicates it. After all, recent history shows that representational pictures are to be evaluated in a way that is not appropriate for non-representational paintings. The chapters that follow still promise an account of the evaluation of representational pictures as representational.

Setting Newman and Hoffman aside is more likely to mean a missed opportunity than a mistake. There is little well-developed philosophical discussion of paintings like Newman's and Hoffman's, and giving them serious thought may prove the only way to achieve some insights into the evaluation of pictures as vehicles for seeing-in. However, it is just as likely that evaluating these paintings for what they are either has little to do with their sustaining seeing-in or provides few clues to the evaluation of pictures that do sustain seeing-in.

A second limitation of the book is trumpeted in the first word of its title. According to the mimesis thesis, pictures typically elicit experiences as of the scenes they depict, which experiences resemble, in important respects, face-to-face experiences of the same scenes. Notice that this claim is neutral as regards the sense modality of the scene-presenting experiences that pictures typically elicit. It does not presuppose, in particular, that the experiences are visual—mediated by sight. Although this presupposition seems incontestable, it is in fact false. Some pictures are made of raised lines standing for objects' outlines, and touching the raised lines typically elicits scene-presenting experiences in blind and sighted people alike (Kennedy 1993). The experiences are cases not of seeing-in but rather of perceiving-in.

Tactile pictures suggest that pictures are not exclusively visual and that their visuality is a special case of a more generic spatial perception (Lopes 1997, 2002; Hopkins 2000). The mimesis thesis can accommodate this suggestion because it is neutral about sense modality.

In addition, tactile pictures prompt speculation about the aesthetic evaluation of pictures. If visual pictures are evaluated for their visual features, then tactile pictures may be evaluated for their tactile features. In so far as the two sets of features are not coextensive, there are two classes of pictorial evaluation—the tactile and the visual. When the two classes overlap, some features may be more salient in one modality than the other—textures are more salient in touch than vision, for example. Thus experiences of pictures in one modality may refocus attention on experiences of pictures in the other modality. None of these possibilities is blocked by the pictorial evaluation thesis, which is also neutral as to sense modality.

For all that, this book discusses only visual pictures and the experiences of seeing-in that they afford. Although tactile pictures exist in the thousands, most are maps, textbook illustrations, or instructional diagrams that are not typically targets of aesthetic evaluation—at least, not consciously so. Moreover, few tactile pictures have been designed as objects of aesthetic attention, so almost all the pictures that anyone evaluates aesthetically are visual. Nobody can say what the future holds, and tactile pictures may become regular objects of aesthetic evaluation—there are reasons to believe that the possibility is a live one (Lopes 1997, 2002). None the less, we may only speculate about the details of the aesthetic evaluation of tactile pictures as vehicles for perceiving-in.

The exclusion of tactile pictures is a special case of a more general exclusion. As should be abundantly clear, *Sight and Sensibility* concerns the aesthetic and non-aesthetic evaluation of pictures *as vehicles for seeing-in*, to the exclusion of all other evaluations of pictures, aesthetic and otherwise. Evaluations of pictures as formal constructions, as the products of intentional processes of making, and as historically and socially embedded artefacts are left out.

Exclusion does not imply pre-eminence, however. The account given in the chapters that follow is admittedly partial, and does not answer all the questions one might have about pictures and the evaluation of them. Pictures are obviously much more than vehicles for seeing-in, and many are barely interesting if viewed as such— their value lies elsewhere. This, then, is a third limitation of the book. It is one worth accepting if a partial account is a good first step towards a full account.

A fourth and final caveat has to do with the art question. We should not assume that an account, full or partial, of the evaluation of pictures is an account of the evaluation of pictures as art. Chapter 3 argues that aesthetic evaluation is not reducible to art evaluation. Beyond this, it is a matter of some dispute whether there is any logical connection between aesthetic evaluation and art evaluation— whether, for instance, artistic merit implies aesthetic merit. *Sight and Sensibility* does not offer a theory of the value of pictorial art.

Accepting this limitation has advantages and disadvantages. An advantage is that in developing a conception of pictorial visuality and in defending interactionism we may look to artworks and non-artworks alike. After all, art is a recent phenomenon not found in all cultures, and pictorial artworks are vastly outnumbered by non-art pictures. True, many artists have set about making pictures with high aesthetic merit, so we may expect the cases that come most readily to mind to be works of art—indeed the finest works of art, such as pictures by Vermeer and Degas. At the same time, it is wise to remember that much recent (if not *very* recent) art production and thinking about art have been informed by a doctrinaire autonomism. Many artists have made works on the assumption that there is no route to aesthetic merit by way of cognitive or moral merit. This makes for a biased sample that is corrected by attention to non-art pictures.

A disadvantage of making a turn toward the aesthetic bypassing the artistic is that we deprive ourselves of the many arguments constructed by philosophers during the past decade for and against interaction between artistic and non-artistic value (Carroll 1996; Jacobson 1997; Anderson and Dean 1998; Gaut 1998; Stecker 2005). Some of these philosophers argue that moral evaluations of works of art can count for or against findings of artistic merit. Supposing them to be successful, these arguments support aesthetic interactionism only if findings of artistic merit or demerit imply findings of aesthetic merit or demerit. We should not lament missing this short cut to interactionism: artistic interactionism is no less disputed than its aesthetic cousin.

The approach of this book is expressed in its title and in the two assumptions from which it springs: the mimesis thesis and the pictorial evaluation thesis. In fact, the approach is an ancient one: starting from a conception of pictorially mediated experience, Plato notoriously argued in book 10 of the *Republic* that pictures can have little merit. *Sight and Sensibility* takes Plato's method in the opposite direction. It uses a conception of pictorially mediated experience to defend a more optimistic view of aesthetic evaluation.

1 THE PUZZLE OF MIMESIS

For don't you mark? We're made so that we love
First when we see them painted, things we have passed
Perhaps a hundred times nor cared to see.

Robert Browning

According to the pictorial evaluation thesis, to evaluate a picture as a picture is, in part, to evaluate it as eliciting experiences of the scene it depicts. According to the mimesis thesis, pictures typically elicit experiences as of the scenes they depict, which experiences resemble, in important respects, face-to-face experiences of the same scenes. For example, a picture of an old pair of shoes typically elicits an experience like one of seeing an old pair of shoes face to face, and to evaluate the picture as a picture is in part to evaluate it as a vehicle for seeing some old shoes. However, the pictorial evaluation and mimesis theses generate a puzzle when taken together. Solving the puzzle means giving the mimesis thesis the right interpretation.

A Puzzle

Reflecting on van Gogh's *Pair of Shoes* (Fig. 3), Flint Schier observes that 'a pair of old boots is not normally an object of lively aesthetic, moral or epistemic suggestion' and then asks 'why...should van Gogh's painting of boots hold our interest?' (1993: 176). If a picture shows how a scene looks, then how can an evaluation of it diverge from an evaluation of an experience of the scene face to face? How, for example, can anyone be moved by a picture-induced experience of some old shoes unless they are also moved by an experience of the shoes seen face to face?

Fig. 3. Vincent van Gogh, *A Pair of Shoes*, 1886. Photo credit: Art Resource, NY.

These questions expose a tension between the mimesis and pictorial evaluation theses. We may doubt that an evaluation of a picture responds to its mimetic content if a positive evaluation of the picture is left standing despite the fact that face-to-face experience of the depicted scene is not worth having. Either pictures are not mimetic, contrary to the mimesis thesis, or evaluations of them need not take account of their mimetic content, contrary to the pictorial evaluation thesis.

The puzzle seems to dissolve if we have in mind only pictures depicting scenes worth seeing face to face. Turner's *Heidelberg Sunset* is worth looking at because sunsets are worth looking at.

In fact, cases like the Turner compound the puzzle. Some pictures are worth looking at, and depict objects that are worth looking at, though the latter does not fully account for the former. As part of a longer defence of the value of depiction, Alberti wrote that 'you can conceive of almost nothing so precious which is not made far richer and much more beautiful by association with painting. Ivory, gems and similar expensive things become more precious when worked by the hand of the painter' (1966: 64). Alberti overstates his case: a piece of ivory is not as a rule any more precious for having been depicted. What is true is that there is often something extra to be gained from seeing something in a picture, however precious the experience of seeing it face to face. A sunset is worth lingering over, but a picture of it may doubly deserve sustained and intense scrutiny.

This fact suggests another way to resolve the puzzle of mimesis. Perhaps scenes are worth seeing in pictures because pictures depict them as having visually interesting features that they are not seen to have face to face. Apples and pears captivate the eye when made to look as Chardin or Cézanne make them look.

Although in many cases the puzzle dissolves for this reason, the subjects of a great many pictures we value highly scarcely reward attention when seen face to face. *A Pair of Shoes* illustrates the point perfectly, for it steadfastly refuses to idealize or prettify or in any way dress up its subject. It shows shoes as ordinary, not to elevate the ordinary but simply to portray it in all its ordinariness. So although some pictures depict what we cannot otherwise see, many depict what is already boringly before our eyes. It is no puzzle that pictures should be valued for making visible the invisible; the puzzle is that they should be valued for repeating what is already all around us.

The puzzle is not solved by pointing out that there are factors pertinent to the evaluation of pictures as pictures that have nothing to do with their mimetic function. We value pictures for purely formal characteristics of their surfaces—as arrangements of colours, shapes, and textures not seen as depicting any scene. A picture might accrue value because of its history (Picasso made it at the age of 3) or its historical impact (it changed people's attitudes).

While true, these observations miss the point. The pictorial evaluation thesis does not say that pictures are to be evaluated as pictures *only* for their mimetic content. It is consistent with the observation that non-mimetic features of a picture can compensate for or add to its eliciting a scene-presenting experience.

Schier asks 'what does van Gogh's art *add* to the mere experience of looking at boots in order to make the experience of looking at his painting a moving and important one?' (1993: 176, emphasis added). Although this is a legitimate question, whose answer contributes to a full account of the factors properly at play in evaluating pictures, it side-steps the puzzle of mimesis. Van Gogh's painting is moving partly for its inducing an experience as of looking at old shoes. Yet, looking at old shoes is not moving. It is here that the puzzle grips us, and we cannot be released by enumerating non-mimetic features of pictures that compensate for their humdrum subject-matter.

In sum, the puzzle of mimesis arises so long as some pictures are worth looking at *partly in so far as they prompt scene-presenting experiences* and yet face-to-face experiences of the same scenes are less worth having.

Hints of a better solution are dropped by Aristotle and Hutcheson, who attribute the value of pictures to a delight in depiction (Aristotle 1987; Hutcheson 1973: sect. 4). There is something to this: we do delight in the fact that a flat surface cleverly evokes an experience as of a depicted scene. However, one obvious way to interpret the proposal is implausible, and the other reinforces the puzzle.

On a strong reading of Aristotle and Hutcheson, pictorial mimesis is valuable in itself, and this explains the advantage that seeing shoes in *A Pair of Shoes* enjoys over seeing shoes in one's closet (as well as the value added to depictions of scenes that are already worth seeing). However, we do not value just any success in evoking scene-presenting experiences. Having graciously inspected dozens of your friends' baby pictures, you are unlikely to be delighted by their excellence as likenesses. Aristotle and Hutcheson lived at a time when images were prized as technical achievements; ours is a world awash in cheaply produced, highly effective examples of mimesis.

On a weak reading of Aristotle and Hutcheson, we take delight in only some, successful depiction. This is true, but it hardly solves the puzzle of mimesis. After all, it raises the question of what counts as success in depiction. Some pictures are successful in so far as they prompt experiences of scenes that are less worth seeing face to face. The explanation is not that they are depictive and that depiction itself delights, if not all depiction delights.

To solve the puzzle, we must recognize some salient differences between the experiences involved in seeing in pictures and in face-to-face seeing. First, pictures can depict scenes that, occurring in the past or in the future or in some fictional world, cannot be seen face to face. Second, those that do depict what can be seen face to face may nevertheless reveal facets of their subjects not revealed by seeing them face to face. Third, we interpret pictures in ways that we do not interpret ordinary perceptions, so pictures may convey additional messages by means of the scenes they depict. These facts complicate but do not impeach the mimesis thesis, for difference is at home with similarity. The challenge is to specify how seeing a thing in a picture is at once significantly similar to and also significantly different from seeing it in the flesh.

The differences must be differences in the scene-presenting experiences involved in seeing things in pictures, on the one hand, and seeing things face to face, on the other. A person who sees O in a picture has an O-presenting experience, but she may also have an O-presenting experience by seeing O face to face. It does not follow, of course, that seeing-in and seeing face to face are identical. One is seeing a picture and seeing some scene by seeing the picture; the other is not—it is at most seeing a picture face to face without seeing a scene by means of it. This is not the difference we seek. Resolving the puzzle of mimesis requires an account of how seeing-in and seeing face to face are different and similar *in respect of the scene-presenting experiences they involve*. That one experience is part of seeing-in and another is part of naked-eye seeing is not entirely irrelevant, though. The differences and similarities we seek run deep, because they are consequences of, and so help explain, the fact that in one case the scene-presenting experience is part of seeing-in whereas in the other case it is part of seeing face to face.

Content, Design, and Subject

Caution must be exercised from the first, so as not to confuse the mimesis thesis with a resemblance theory of depiction. In philosophy, caution often takes the form of making distinctions.

A picture is a two-dimensional surface that depicts a scene in virtue of the way its surface is marked and coloured. Use 'design' to refer to those visible surface properties in virtue of which a picture depicts what it does. Design comprises the surface configurations that you see when you see the picture surface without seeing anything in it and that are responsible for your seeing something in it. Not every intrinsic visible property of a picture surface is part of its design, however. We may be able to see that a picture is made of canvas or is very old, but if these are not features in virtue of which the picture depicts what it does, then they are not elements of its design.

Representational pictures also have subjects—the (sometimes fictional) objects, scenes, or events they depict. The subject of *Mont Ste-Victoire* is the Provençal mountain; the subject of the *Flaying of Marsyas* is a fictional or mythic event involving Marsyas and Apollo.

Distinct from both a picture's design and its subject is its content, the properties it represents its subject as having. A common error is to identify content with subject—to identify properties a picture represents the world as having with properties the world has. This misses the fact that any picture may misrepresent, depicting its subject as having properties it does not have. That an image depicts Sean Connery as red-haired does not entail that he has red hair.

Finally, the content of a picture should be distinguished from the content of the scene-presenting experiences it triggers. The latter normally depends on the former—you normally see a bowl of flowers in a picture only if that is what it depicts—but the two contents can come apart, if the picture is hard to see clearly, for example, or if the viewer's visual system malfunctions. In situations like this, there is no saying how what is seen in a picture arises from what it depicts.

Armed with these distinctions, we can see why the mimesis thesis does not entail a resemblance theory of depiction. According to such theories, a picture's content, when accurate, is determined in part by a resemblance between its design and its subject. A proponent of such a theory is C. S. Peirce, who defines the iconic by appeal to a resemblance between sensible properties of the icon and of the object in nature that it represents:

> an icon is a *representamen* of what it represents ... by virtue of its being an immediate image, that is to say by virtue of characters which belong to it in itself as a sensible object, and which it would possess just the same were there no object in nature that it resembled ... it simply happens that its qualities resemble those of the object. (1931: 447)

A picture depicts a bowl of flowers because its design resembles a bowl of flowers.

Fatal difficulties have made resemblance theories historical curiosities. What is important to note is that, if the mimesis thesis is correct, a resemblance obtains between (1) the scene-presenting experiences a picture elicits and (2) experiences of the picture's subject in the flesh. This resemblance is not identical and does entail a resemblance between (3) the picture's design and (4) its subject. It is one thing to say that seeing an object in a picture is similar to seeing it in the flesh; it is another to say that the picture's design-constituting marks and colourations resemble features of the object. Denying a resemblance between (3) and (4) is no bar to accepting that there is a resemblance between (1) and (2).

A variant on resemblance theories does have contemporary advocates. According to the variant, a picture accurately depicts an object only if its spectators *experience* salient features of its design as similar to salient features of the object. What features are salient is difficult to know, and several suggestions have been made (Peacocke 1987; Budd 1993; Hopkins 1998). There is no present need to look into the details; any viable version of the experienced resemblance theory is committed to two claims that are relevant here.

The first is that the content of seeing-in is complex. A picture does not merely elicit an experience as of the depicted scene; it elicits a tripartite experience of a resemblance between salient design features and salient features of the subject. Thus people looking at Cézanne's *Mont Ste-Victoire* normally experience a resemblance between parts of it and parts of Mont Ste-Victoire itself. The second claim is that to grasp the content of a picture one must experience this picture–object resemblance. Putting the two claims together, we can tell stories like this: I experience that salient similarity between a picture's design and some flowers, and this is part of my understanding that it depicts the flowers.

Whereas the mimesis thesis posits a resemblance between (1) the scene-presenting experiences that pictures elicit and (2) face-to-face experiences of their subjects, the experienced resemblance theory of depiction posits an experienced resemblance between (3) salient features of a picture's design and (4) salient features of its subject.

The mimesis thesis entails neither claim that is characteristic of experienced resemblance theories. One may insist, for instance, that to see a bowl of flowers in a picture, one need only have an experience as of a bowl of flowers—one need not have an experience of any resemblance between the picture's design and the bowl of flowers. As E. H. Gombrich (1961) taught us, the scene-presenting experience a picture elicits may be similar to the experience its subject elicits even when its design is experienced as vastly dissimilar to its subject. This explains why we can switch back and forth between the two experiences, as one may alternate between the two aspects of the duck–rabbit image. Likewise, it is possible to grant the mimesis thesis, yet deny that grasp of what a picture depicts is constituted by seeing-in; one might hold that what we see in a picture depends on a grasp of what it depicts (Goodman 1976; Lopes 1996, 2003*b*; Hyman 2000).

It would be a mistake to dismiss experienced resemblance theories as irrelevant to the task of characterizing seeing-in. Perhaps the complex content claim is just what we need. Perhaps the best way to characterize the relationship between seeing O in a picture and seeing O in the flesh is to take seeing O in a picture to involve seeing a resemblance between the picture and O. The suggestion is taken up at the end of the chapter.

It would be surprising if the mimesis thesis by itself implied any theory of depiction. The aim of a theory of depiction is to explain what it is for a picture to have content, but the mimesis thesis takes for granted that a picture has a given content—a content that is typically the content of seeing-in—and one cannot take for granted what one hopes to explain. For this reason, no plausible theory of depiction may make a mystery of pictorial mimesis. Even 'symbol' theories of depiction, such as Nelson Goodman's, attempt to explain pictorial mimesis—in Goodman's case as a consequence of the entrenchment of the symbol system to which a picture belongs (1976: 34–9). The fact that we see things in pictures cannot help us to choose between plausible theories of depiction.

Seeing Divided, Seeing Double

When we look at a picture, we normally see in it the scene it depicts, but we may also see its design as a design. Of course, there is a sense in which we always see a picture's design when we see things in it, for we always see a scene in a picture by seeing the picture face to face. It is only in virtue of seeing the configuration of marks on its surface, and being sensitive to visible changes in them, that we see anything at all in the picture. However, seeing a pictorial design face to face does not entail seeing the design as a design—it does not entail

design seeing: a visual experience of a picture as a configuration, on a two-dimensional surface, of marks, colours, and textures in virtue of which the surface depicts a scene.

Design seeing is crucial to advanced picture-making abilities, since it amounts to seeing design features as responsible for seeing-in (Fig. 4).

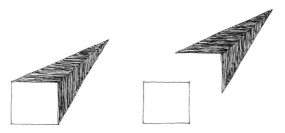

Fig. 4. Design seeing: *left*, a square and its shadow; *right*, when detached from the square, the shadow shape is readily seen to be a flat design shaped like an arrow head.

Thus one way to understand how seeing a scene in a picture diverges from seeing the scene face to face is to consider the relation of seeing-in to design seeing. Unlike seeing-in, face-to-face seeing bears no relation to design seeing, for in face-to-face seeing there is no design to be seen (unless what is seen is a non-depicted designed surface).

Illusion

One conception of the relation between seeing-in and design seeing is a familiar part of E. H. Gombrich's views on art and illusion (1961, 1973). These views have two parts (though they are not usually distinguished). One is an explanation of depiction, and the second is an account of seeing-in.

On the former score Gombrich argues that pictures depict by taking advantage of ambiguities or failures of visual discrimination. A picture depicts a bowl of flowers because the markings on its surface 'fool' the human visual processing system, which responds to the picture as it would when presented with an actual bowl of flowers. This theory of depiction is independent of the second part of Gombrich's view—an account of the relationship between seeing in a picture and seeing its design.

According to Gombrich, seeing-in is illusionistic in the sense that seeing O in a picture and seeing O face to face are phenomenally indistinguishable. The first step in unpacking this proposition is to note that illusion does not require delusion. Seeing a scene in a picture may not cause one to believe that one is seeing the scene in the flesh, and no view that entails otherwise can be correct. Still, there is a connection between illusion and delusion. Whenever seeing O in a picture is phenomenally indistinguishable from seeing O face to face, then seeing O in the picture excludes design seeing, for seeing O face to face is phenomenally distinguishable from design seeing (unless O is a non-depicted picture). But it is only through design seeing that one may see a picture as a picture. So there are circumstances in which those who see O in the picture might, on the basis of this experience, come to believe that they are seeing O face to face.

No doubt viewers sometimes see a picture's design for what it is: namely, a configuration of marks, colours, and textures on its surface that sustain seeing-in. Gombrich proposes that pictorial seeing is always divided between seeing-in and design seeing. We may see a scene in a picture, or we may see the picture's design as a design, but never both at once—much as we may see a duck or a rabbit in the duck–rabbit figure but never both simultaneously. Seeing-in is illusionistic, because it is divided from design seeing. Once a design is seen as a design, there is no chance of delusion (barring widespread perceptual or cognitive breakdown).

The illusion theory of seeing-in comes down to two claims. The first characterizes seeing-in: (1) one sees O in a picture when and only when one's experience as of O when looking at the picture is phenomenally indistinguishable from a face-to-face experience of O. Claim (1) entails the second claim, which asserts that seeing-in and design seeing are divided: (2) in no case can one simultaneously see O in a picture and see the picture's design as a design. Seeing a picture's design as a design is incompatible with seeing O in the picture if the latter is phenomenally indistinguishable from seeing O face to face.

One might ask whether the illusion theory promises a solution to the puzzle of mimesis. No answer stems from the claim that seeing-in is phenomenally indistinguishable from seeing face to face. More promising is the idea that seeing-in differs from seeing face to face in so far as it is divided from, and so can switch over to, design seeing. Unfortunately, Gombrich never explains what contribution switching between seeing old shoes in a canvas and seeing the canvas as a design can make to the evaluation of a picture. We need not speculate until we have considered whether the illusion theory is adequate.

Contrary to (1), the experience involved in seeing-in is not as a rule phenomenally indistinguishable from that involved in plain seeing. The test of phenomenal indistinguishability is that there are circumstances in which the experience would cause one to believe that one really is seeing the depicted scene. It goes without saying that we rarely see a scene in a picture without also seeing the setting in which the picture is displayed—whether it be a gilt frame hanging on a panelled wall or the pages of a magazine—and seeing the setting is enough to counteract the risk of delusion. The difficulty is not insurmountable, because there are ways of displaying pictures (e.g. through pin-holes) so as to mask the setting. More damaging to (1) is the fact that some pictures cannot elicit the required illusion no matter how they are displayed. Line drawings, black and white photographs of coloured objects, and the stylizations of 'primitive' and 'modern' art: there is no way to display these that could lead competent perceivers to believe that they are seeing what is depicted face to face. Seeing-in is not always just like ordinary seeing.

The falsity of (1) removes a reason to believe (2). Is (2) false? Do some pictures allow, or indeed encourage, simultaneous seeing-in and design seeing? Does seeing in pictures divide from design seeing?

It does seem that we can sometimes experience a picture's design as a design and have a scene-presenting experience at one and the same time. Indeed, the duck–rabbit figure undermines Gombrich's intended use of it to illustrate how seeing is divided between seeing-in and design seeing. Switches between the two contents (as of duck and rabbit respectively) are not analogous to switches between the figure's design, on the one hand, and either of its contents, on the other. That duck cannot be seen simultaneously with rabbit fails to show that duck cannot be seen simultaneously with design or design simultaneously with rabbit. On the contrary, one sees the design while seeing in it either duck or rabbit.

Pictures depicting other pictures also indicate that we are some-times able to see a picture's content and its design simultaneously.

Suppose that one picture may depict another in the sense that we see the depicted picture's design and simultaneously see in it the scene that it depicts (Lopes 1996: ch. 11; Newall 2003). That is, suppose that we see the depicted picture as a picture in the depicted scene and not as a window on to a scene beyond. An example is *Woman Holding a Balance* (Fig. 1). Vermeer's painting depicts a painting of the Last Judgement, and we see this *Last Judgement* as a painting—we do not see it as the apocalypse glimpsed through a hole in the wall.

Two explanations of seeing the depicted picture as a picture flow from illusionism.

One is that we see the *Last Judgement's* design as part of seeing the design of *Woman Holding a Balance*. This will not do. If seeing is divided between seeing-in and design seeing, then when we see the design of *Woman Holding a Balance*, we see a configuration of marks, colours, and textures on its surface, and we cannot simultaneously see the *Last Judgement* as depicting the apocalypse, or indeed anything. Unless we see it as depicting something, we do not see it as a picture.

A more plausible explanation is that seeing the design of the *Last Judgement* is part of seeing the *Last Judgement* in *Woman Holding a Balance*. On this hypothesis, both the design of the *Last Judgement* and the apocalypse it depicts are seen in *Woman Holding a Balance*—the latter in virtue of the former. But if seeing in the *Last Judgement* is illu-sionistic, then we cannot see the apocalypse in it and simultaneously see its design. It follows that when we see the apocalypse in the *Last Judgement*, we do not see it as a picture. This consequence contradicts the supposition that we do see the *Last Judgement* as a picture in *Woman Holding a Balance*, not as a hole in the wall behind the woman.

One reply to this dilemma gives up on the initial supposition—that we see the depicted picture as a picture. Perhaps we do see it as a window looking on to a scene beyond. The trouble with this reply is that it collapses a valuable distinction between pictures that depict pictures as pictures and those that depict pictures but not as pictures. An example of the latter is Magritte's *La Condition humaine* (Fig. 5).

Fig. 5. René Magritte, *La Condition humaine*, 1933. © Estate of René Magritte/ADAGP (Paris)/SODRAC (Montréal) 2004. Photo credit: Bridgeman-Giraudon/Art Resource, NY.

It carries off a visual pun that the Vermeer does not, and the pun depends on its being hard to see the picture on the easel as a picture—the signs that it is a picture are kept to a minimum. By contrast, we clearly see the *Last Judgement* hanging on the wall in the Vermeer as a picture. If the supposition we began with is false, we should expect no difference in our experience of the two depicted pictures.

If (1) is false, then we have no reason to believe (2), and if (2) is also false, then we have another reason to doubt (1).

The illusion theory fares better when weakened. Some pictures elicit experiences as of their subjects that are phenomenally indistinguishable from experiences of their subjects seen face to face. Others allow for simultaneous seeing-in and design seeing. Amending (1), the claim is that, in some cases, seeing O in a picture is phenomenally indistinguishable from seeing O face to face. Amending (2), some pictures prohibit simultaneous seeing-in and design seeing. (1) as amended entails (2) as amended: if a picture prompts illusionistic seeing-in, then it cannot allow simultaneous design seeing and seeing-in, for that would defeat the illusion.

Twofoldness

Richard Wollheim's (1980, 1987, 1998) twofoldness account of seeing-in implies that the illusion theory is incorrect even when weakened. According to Wollheim, seeing-in is one component of an experience with two aspects: a simultaneous or 'twofold' experience of design and depicted scene (Wollheim calls the complete, twofold experience 'seeing-in'). It is impossible to see a scene in a picture without also seeing the picture's design as a design. Thus pictures exploit tensions between design shape and depicted shape (e.g. Cézanne's still lifes), design colour and depicted colour (e.g. late works by Titian), or design texture and represented texture (e.g. many oils by van Gogh). An integral part of appreciating these pictures is noticing, attempting to reconcile, and seeking to make sense of the failure to reconcile these tensions. Experiences of the depicted scene and the pictorial design always interpenetrate one another.

If some pictures promote twofold seeing-in and design seeing, then the strong version of the illusion theory is wrong. Nevertheless, weak illusionism is viable unless experiences of pictures are inevitably twofold. Why should anyone believe this stronger proposition?

One reason Wollheim gives is that twofold experience is essential to the evaluation of pictures. The point is premature: we are trying to make sense of the mimesis thesis to set up a discussion of mimetic content as a factor in evaluating pictures.

A second reason is that twofoldness is the best explanation of the constancy of scene-presenting experiences (Wollheim 1980: 215–16). When a picture is viewed from an oblique angle, the shapes we see in it are not distorted, as the laws of optics predict. This is because the visual system corrects for shape using information about the picture's orientation relative to the viewer. So what is seen in a picture depends upon information about its surface.

This reasoning is invalid. Perceptual constancy requires that the visual system access information about the surface of pictures, but it does not follow that the surface is experienced. We may see the design without seeing it *as* a design, if design information is used by vision to correct for viewing position without entering conscious experience. Consider *trompe-l'œil* ceiling painting, where we normally do not see the surface as the surface it is (Fig. 6). True, when these pictures are not viewed from the expected viewpoint, their depicta look distorted. Even so, this shows only that design information is necessary for *constancy in seeing-in*, not for seeing-in. Constancy may fail in seeing-in.

Moreover, were the reasoning valid, it would show only that information about the picture *surface* plays a role in the operation of constancy. Surface is not design, though. A picture's design properties are typically a subset of its visible surface properties. Design seeing represents a configuration of marks, colours, and textures on a two-dimensional surface in virtue of which the surface depicts a scene, but not all visible properties of a picture surface are

Fig. 6. *Trompe-l'œil* dome, St Peter's, Vienna.

ones in virtue of which it depicts a scene. Design seeing should not be confused with

surface seeing: a visual experience of a picture as a configuration of marks, colours, and textures on a two-dimensional surface.

In general, a picture's orientation with respect to a viewer is a property of its surface but not its design, since it is not a property in virtue of which the picture depicts what it does (its content does not change with the viewer's movements, and neither does the content of seeing-in). An explanation of constancy requires at most that constant seeing-in be accompanied by surface seeing, not design seeing.

Troubles with trompe-l'œil

Distinguishing between surface and design seeing makes sense of *trompe-l'œil*, and also indicates that there is more to the weak version of the illusion theory than meets the eye.

The arguments against the strong illusion theory suggest that it assimilates all pictures to *trompe-l'œil*. The theory states that seeing-in is illusionistic in the sense that it necessarily divides from design seeing, and so is phenomenally indistinguishable from face-to-face seeing. The implication is that for any picture there are circumstances in which design seeing is suppressed and seeing O in a picture engenders the belief that one is seeing O face to face. For most pictures these circumstances are unusual, involving pin-holes and other special devices. In *trompe-l'œil*, the required circumstances are not unusual—they are the circumstances of normal viewing. What distinguishes *trompe-l'œil* pictures from other pictures is merely that the former may delude in ordinary viewing conditions, whereas the latter require special circumstances, and this is not a difference in principle. If this is not a difference in principle, the arguments against illusionism seem to show that no pictures are illusionistic.

As we have seen, however, the division of seeing-in from design seeing is not sufficient to explain *trompe-l'œil*. A picture may only *trompe l'œil* when it suppresses not just design seeing but also surface seeing, for seeing face to face is not surface seeing (unless what is seen face to face is an undepicted picture). Thus pictures painted on inaccessible surfaces such as the ceiling in Figure 6 generate the most robust and impressive *trompe-l'œil* effects. There are two ways to see an illusionistic picture as a picture. One may see the depicted scene in it while seeing its surface: that is not to see how the illusion is pulled off. Seeing how the illusion is pulled off requires design seeing.

If the division of seeing-in from surface seeing is necessary for illusion or *trompe-l'œil* and if the division of seeing-in from design seeing is not sufficient to divide seeing-in from surface seeing, then some non-illusionistic pictures may divide seeing-in from design seeing.

Weak illusionism predicts this. The view comprises two claims. First, in some cases, seeing O in a picture is phenomenally indistin-guishable from seeing O face to face. Second, in some pictures seeing-in is divided from design seeing. This second claim allows that some pictures divide seeing-in from design seeing and are not illusionistic (they fail under any circumstances to *trompe l'œil*) because they double seeing-in with surface seeing.

We should therefore expect divided seeing to be more common than the rarity of *trompe-l'œil* suggests. Some pictures support something like illusionistic seeing-in—call it 'naturalism'. We see the surface of such a picture as a surface even as we see a scene in it, but we cannot see anything in it while we see its design as a design. The depicted scene is seen with the surface, but how the former emerges from the latter is not seen. This is the point of Gombrich's story about Kenneth Clark's experience of a Velázquez:

he wanted to observe what went on when the brush-strokes and dabs of pigment on the canvas transformed themselves into visions of transfigured reality as he stepped back. But try as he might, stepping forward or backward, he could never hold both visions at the same time, and therefore, the answer to his problem of how it was done always seemed to elude him. (1961: 6)

Clark may continue to see the surface; but what he cannot see, as long as he sees the depicted scene, is how that surface depicts the scene—he cannot see the surface as a design.

Trompe-l'œil makes trouble for the twofoldness theory. Wollheim admits that if our experiences of pictures must double seeing-in with design seeing, then *trompe-l'œils* are not pictures. Presumably the thought is that no representation is a picture unless it is normally seen as one, and seeing a picture as a picture requires design seeing as well as seeing-in.

This admission reverses intuitions about pictures and controverts a conception of depiction that has guided and continues to guide the production of a great many pictures: namely, those in which illusion is an ideal. However, one person's *modus tollens* is another's *modus ponens*. One might bite the bullet segregating illusionistic imaging from depiction (e.g. Feagin 1998).

No matter. The distinction between design and surface seeing exposes a damaging ambiguity in the claim that to experience a picture as a picture is to have a twofold experience.

Twofold experience may double seeing-in with surface seeing but not with design seeing. In that case, *trompe-l'œil* images are pictures because they sometimes allow seeing-in to double with surface seeing, and it is only in special circumstances (e.g. when they are painted on high ceilings) that they suppress seeing their surfaces and thereby threaten to induce delusion. After all, *trompe-l'œil* pictures deliver a special pleasure in seeing that what a moment ago looked to be a frolic of putti is in fact, as one now sees, a painted plane.

Alternatively, twofold experience may be taken to require that seeing-in double with design seeing. A strong case is required for this claim, since naturalistic pictures divide seeing-in from design seeing, and naturalistic depiction is common. Moreover, the case must hinge on the distinction between mere surface seeing and more sophisticated design seeing.

An obvious argument is that unless one simultaneously sees the depicted scene and the depicting design, one cannot see how the latter undergirds the former and how the former is an elaboration of the latter, and seeing a picture as a picture amounts to seeing its undergirding—to seeing, as it were, the process of depiction and not merely its product.

Is this argument sound? Why must seeing-in and design seeing occur simultaneously? Why can we not see how design grounds content and content elaborates design by switching from one to the other?

It is plausible that no representation is a picture unless it provides for its being seen as one, but double seeing-in and surface seeing, which is allowed even by *trompe-l'œil* images, meets this condition. Ruling out *trompe-l'œil* by requiring seeing-in to double with design seeing also rules out non-illusionistic pictures which we always experience as pictures.

Ways of seeing-in

Some pictures encourage double seeing-in and design seeing—they wear the process of depiction on their sleeves and so are not illusionistic. Some pictures divide seeing-in from design seeing but

Table 1. *The varieties of seeing-in*

Seeing-in	Illusionistic	Non-illusionistic
Divided from design seeing	*Trompe-l'œil*	Naturalism Pseudo-twofoldness
Doubled with design seeing	Actualism?	Twofoldness

not surface seeing—they obscure the process of depiction, and yet we see them as pictures. Other pictures are illusionistic because they divide seeing-in from design seeing and in some circumstances from surface seeing too. When characterized in relation to design seeing and surface seeing, seeing-in is a plural phenomenon. The plurality has a structure, however. Seeing-in may be illusionistic or not; and it may double with design seeing or not. The options are represented in Table 1.

The strong version of the illusion theory restricts seeing-in to the top left, and the twofoldness theory restricts seeing-in to the bottom right. Naturalism puts pressure on both strong illusionism and the twofoldness theory. Naturalistic pictures are not illusionistic, since they always double with surface seeing and so are apprehended as pictures. At the same time, they defeat twofold seeing-in—seeing the depicted scene blocks seeing their designs. This mapping of the possibility space has more to offer, however.

Wollheim holds that we always see a picture's design at the same time as we see in it the scene it depicts: the one interpenetrates the other in a single experience. Design seeing transforms the content of seeing-in so that it no longer matches the content of seeing the scene face to face. Design is 'recruited' into the depicted scene so that the scene no longer looks the way it would when seen face to face (Podro 1998: 13).

Can properties of the depicted scene be recruited, in the other direction, to transform design seeing? The design of Picasso's *Portrait of Daniel-Henry Kahnweiler* acquires a new appearance once you see Kahnweiler in it. Otherwise disparate regions of the picture surface come to look organized into a whole that looks responsible for depicting Kahnweiler. It seems that the content of seeing-in informs design seeing.

However, there is an asymmetry between the recruitment of design seeing to seeing-in, on the one hand, and the recruitment of seeing-in to design seeing, on the other. Features of design determine the features the subject is depicted as having, but features the subject is depicted as having cannot determine the picture's design. The reason is that the design features of a picture are by definition those in virtue of which it depicts what it does. Our seeing them explains how we come to see anything in the picture. As a result, they must be visible independently of seeing anything in the picture. Therefore, seeing the surface as having features which can only be seen in it as a result of seeing something in that surface cannot count as design seeing.

The phenomenon of subjective contour illustrates the point economically. Consider the famous image of the Dalmatian (Fig. 7),

Fig. 7. Dalmatian.

whose characteristic colouring is echoed in the dappled light on the ground and realized in a random-looking arrangement of ink spots. When you see the dog in the image, you see a contour in the ink spots that matches the dog's outline, but when you see no dog in the image, the contour dissolves into a patchwork of unrelated blobs. That is, seeing the ink spots as having that contour depends upon seeing the dog in the image. It is tempting to describe the situation as one in which what is seen in the image—a doggy outline—is recruited as an element of the image's design—the contour. This is a mistake. Seeing the contour is a part of seeing the dog, and does not explain how the dog comes to be seen in the picture. Therefore, the contour is not a design feature, and seeing it is not design seeing.

The Dalmatian image strikingly illustrates a more widespread phenomenon. Effects like subjective contour are deliberately exploited by picture-makers—they are as much a part of the resources of the medium as line, colour, and shading.

Seeing-in is sometimes pseudo-twofold, doubled not with design seeing but with pseudo-design seeing—seeing the picture surface as having properties that seem to be design properties but are not in fact properties in virtue of which it depicts what it does. Pictures like the Dalmatian and *Kahnweiler* require a Gombrichian switch if their actual designs are to be seen. Thus pseudo-twofoldness is close kin to naturalism. In both, seeing-in is divided from design seeing yet non-illusionistic. Like naturalism, pseudo-twofoldness gives us reason to reject the strong illusion and twofoldness theories of seeing-in.

Can illusionistic seeing-in double with design seeing? It can, if we suppose that a picture can depict what it is. Consider Jasper Johns's paintings of targets. Seeing the target in the picture is evidently illusionistic, for seeing the picture is phenomenally indistinguishable from seeing a target. The picture *is* a target! So if, as we have supposed, we see a target in the picture, then we simultaneously see the painting's surface, including properties of the surface in virtue of which we see the target. After all, properties of the surface are properties of the target: if the painting's surface is crumbly or garish, for example, so is the surface of the target. We could not see properties of one without seeing the other. In sum, seeing the target in the picture is phenomenally indistinguishable from seeing a target face to face and also doubles with seeing the picture's design. Granting the supposition that the picture depicts a target, it doubles illusionistic seeing-in with design seeing. Pictures like Johns's target painting may be labelled 'actualist'.

Should we grant the supposition we can see O in a picture that is an O? Can a picture depict what it is? Answering this question is the task of a theory of depiction. At least a pluralist conception of seeing-in more tolerant than strong illusionism, and the twofoldness theory is agnostic on the question, for it rules out neither double seeing nor illusionism.

Experienced resemblance

It is time to return to experienced resemblance theories of seeing-in (Peacocke 1987; Budd 1993; Hopkins 1998). These theories are widely accepted, but they are inconsistent with a pluralist account of seeing-in.

According to experienced resemblance theories, our experiences of pictures are experiences of resemblances between designs and depicted scenes. Seeing Mont Ste-Victoire in *Mont Ste-Victoire* is seeing one thing—the painting's design—as resembling another—the mountain itself.

This is a generic characterization; individual theories specify different respects in which the resemblance obtains. Malcolm Budd proposes that design is experienced as resembling the visual field representation of the depicted scene when it is seen from some point of view, where the 'visual field' is the 'visual world considered in abstraction from one of its three spatial dimensions, namely distance outward from [one's] point of view' (1993: 158). Robert Hopkins proposes that design is experienced as resembling depicted scene in outline shape, where the outline shape of an object is the set of directions it subtends from a point of view (1998, 2005). Happily, there is no need to consider these proposals in detail.

All experienced resemblance theories of seeing-in imply that seeing-in necessarily doubles with design seeing. Proponents of the theories assume that Wollheim's twofoldness account of seeing-in is correct and use the notion of experienced resemblance to unpack what it is for seeing-in and design seeing to double and interpenetrate each other. Budd makes the point explicit by comparing seeing-in to hearing a variation on a musical theme:

> when you see what is pictured in the surface you see a relation between it and objects of the kind depicted, in a similar sense to that in which you hear a relation between one theme and another when you hear it as a variation of another.... this is what your hearing the relation with the theme consists in. (1993: 161)

Like hearing a musical passage as a variation upon a theme, seeing-in is twofold.

Thus, bracketing the possibility of actualism, experienced resemblance theories imply that seeing O in P is always phenomenally distinguishable from seeing O face to face. Seeing-in is seeing a resemblance between a design and a scene. By contrast, seeing a scene face to face is not ordinarily an experience of it as resembling a design, because there is no design to see (unless one is seeing an undepicted picture).

Again bracketing actualism, three kinds of counterexamples challenge experienced resemblance theories of seeing-in: *trompe-l'œil* images, naturalistic images, and images sustaining pseudo-twofoldness. Any one will do. The Dalmatian image (Fig. 7) is interesting because it might not seem at first glance to provide a counterexample. The subjective contour *is*, after all, experienced as resembling the outline of a dog.

On the contrary, the image doubles seeing-in with seeing a *pseudo*-design. Its design comprises features of its surface in virtue of which we see a dog in it. The doggy outline is not part of the picture's design, since it is a consequence of seeing a dog in the picture and does not explain how we come to see the dog there. That is, since no dog-shaped contour can be seen on the picture surface independently of seeing a dog in the picture, there is no dog-shaped contour on the picture surface in virtue of which we see the dog in the surface. We might experience a resemblance between the outline of a dog and the subjective contour, but that is not an experience of resemblance between the dog's shape and the picture's design.

Pure and impure seeing-in

The varieties of seeing-in make for a variety among pictures, but also for a variety within pictures. Seeing in a picture need not be purely *trompe-l'œil*, naturalistic, pseudo-twofold, twofold, or actualist. Imagine a picture depicting a deep, rippling, reflective, rectangular, blue pool of water. Seeing in the picture may be *trompe-l'œil* with respect to the pool's depth, naturalistic with respect to its rippled surface, pseudo-twofold with respect to its reflectiveness, twofold with respect to its rectangular shape, and actualist with respect to its blue colour. It is an open question how any given determinable can be seen in a picture. Is depicted colour always the same as surface colour, for instance? The important point is that seeing-in takes many forms, not only in different pictures but also within one and the same picture. Pure *trompe-l'œil* is an esoteric phenomenon, and pure actualism may entail the objectionable supposition that a picture may depict what it is. Many pictures, however, mix actualistic or *trompe-l'œil* seeing-in with other varieties of seeing-in. This is a fact that purist accounts of seeing-in cannot explain.

Recognition and Recruitment

Some pictures, some of the time, cause experiences phenomenally indistinguishable from experiences of their subjects seen in the flesh. They normally require us to switch between seeing the depicted scene and seeing their designs (possible exceptions are actualist images like the Johns target). Other pictures elicit scene-presenting experiences that could not be caused by their subjects seen face to face: some double seeing-in with design seeing, and some double seeing-in with surface seeing while dividing seeing-in from design seeing. Nevertheless, all are mimetic. Even non-illusionistic pictures show how things look.

What does it mean to say that a picture shows how O looks, when seeing O in the picture is not just like seeing O face to face? What connects seeing O in the picture and seeing O face to face, when they are not phenomenally indistinguishable? Why is it a mistake to connect what I see in *Mona Lisa* with seeing my dog, Nico, climbing a ladder? Well, obviously, they do not look alike! True, but we have discovered that seeing O in a picture may not match seeing O face to face.

The answer lies in the principle that seeing an object in a picture depends upon and expresses knowledge of the object's appearance. For any object that a picture depicts, one cannot see the object in the picture unless one knows what the object looks like. Of course, knowing what an object looks like need not *pre-date* seeing it in a picture; it might be *obtained* by seeing it in a picture. Not knowing what a satyr looks like, your experience of Titian's *Flaying of Marsyas* may endow you with the knowledge you lacked. Not knowing what Pope Leo looks like, you may learn his appearance with the aid of a portrait of him. In each case, seeing O in a picture entails and expresses knowledge of O's visual appearance.

We need not take a narrow view of what constitutes 'knowledge of what the object looks like'. In particular, there is no reason to think that having knowledge of appearance entails having an experience of the object identical in content to one that might be caused by the object when seen face to face.

The knowledge requirement is met if seeing-in includes the exercise of a visual concept of the depicted object, where a visual concept of O is an ability to reliably identify O by its visual appearance in varying circumstances. The concept may be one which the viewer already possesses, as when he sees a Dalmatian in a picture partly because he knows that *that* is how Dalmatians look; or it may be a concept acquired as a result of seeing in the picture, as when a viewer learns to identify the FBI's Most Wanted person by seeing her in a mug shot. In either case, the ability to recognize objects by their appearance does not require that their appearance never changes. Identifiability by appearance does not imply identity of appearance. One task of vision is to enable us to identify objects as they change. We recognize three-dimensional objects seen from new viewpoints; we recognize faces as they age; we recognize objects transformed in myriad ways by picture-makers. Not only do we recognize objects *despite* these differences; we recognize objects *in* different views of them. We recognize an object as the same as one seen previously, and we also see how it has changed since we saw it last.

In sum, seeing an object in a picture involves knowledge of the object's appearance embodied in a concept of the object enabling the knower to recognize the object under a variety of conditions, notably in the special condition of seeing in pictures. Seeing O in a non-illusionistic picture is an extension of an ability to recognize O in the flesh: O is depicted as having some properties that it could not be seen to have face to face, but it is recognized despite this change in its appearance. Seeing O in a picture connects to seeing O face to face when both involve the exercise of a visual concept of O.

The extensibility of recognition is no impediment to seeing-in. Picture-makers capitalize on the capacity of pictures for showing how things look. They use the resources of the pictorial medium—a flat surface that can be marked and coloured in various ways—in order to extend and elaborate recognition. They do not, as Michael Podro puts it, 'set out to show the look of the world as something previously known, but rather to extend the thread of recognition in new and complex structures of their own' (1998 : p.vii).

This conclusion marks the first step toward solving the puzzle of mimesis—the puzzle of how it is possible for pictures to be worth looking at partly in so far as they prompt scene-presenting experiences when face-to-face experiences of the same scenes would not be worth having. Solving the puzzle requires an explanation of how seeing a thing in a picture is at once significantly similar to and also significantly different from seeing it in the flesh. When it is illusionistic, seeing-in alternates with design or surface seeing. When it is not illusionistic, it doubles with design or surface seeing. In all cases, seeing-in and seeing face to face involve the application of a visual concept of the object seen. Still, the puzzle of mimesis is not yet solved. It remains to consider how pictures are properly evaluated as vehicles for seeing-in.

2 THE 'AIR' OF PICTURES

And I must borrow every changing shape
To find expression ...

T. S. Eliot

Evaluating pictures as pictures requires seeing them and thereby seeing in them the scenes they depict. As part of this, we normally see in them the emotions, feelings, and moods the scenes express. Expression therefore gives rise to an analogue of the puzzle of mimesis. Daumier's drawing entitled *Fatherly Discipline* (Fig. 8) is worth looking at partly because it expresses frustration, impotent shock, and compassion. Yet we do not value in the same way experiences of frustrated people. This is puzzling as long as experiences of pictures expressing frustration are importantly like experiences of people expressing frustration. If pictorial expression is mimetic, then the puzzle of mimesis leads us to ask how seeing what a picture expresses is like and unlike seeing what a person expresses.

Conceptions and Cases

The first step is to narrow what is meant by 'expression'. For example, expression has been singled out as defining art pictures, but some non-art pictures express emotions, and some art pictures express none—there are art traditions which quite intelligibly make inexpressive pictures the ideal. Expression is a resource of depiction and is not definitive of pictorial art: a theory of expression in art is not an expression theory of art. Moving beyond the expression theory of pictorial art, there remain several notions of expression, some quite broad, some more narrow, each more or less compatible with the others.

Fig. 8. Honoré Daumier, *Fatherly Discipline*, 1851–2. Reproduction, The Art Institute of Chicago.

Expression theory

Philosophers have had little to say about expression in pictures (the exception is Wollheim 1993). They have had a lot to say about *musical* expression, and one might extrapolate from music to pictures, but the move is risky if we are interested in evaluating pictures as mimetic representations, for music is not typically mimetic. To get our bearings, we do better to look to landmark discussions in art theory.

The broadest notion of expression used in art theory is twinned with the expression theory of art. Here the meaning of 'expression' reflects its role in establishing that all art, and only art, is expression. One idea is that expression is an artistic act—the act, properly viewed against the backdrop of the artist's life and times, of making the work of art (e.g. Julian Bell 1999: 133–72). The artist expresses something in making the artwork.

Even should this notion of expression prove coherent, it may be set aside. Any appeal that the notion has apart from its alliance with the expression theory of art attaches to a conception of pictures as artefacts whose value derives from their creation. If pictures do have value as things created, this is not relevant to understanding their evaluation as mimetic. Moreover, while creativity may be motivated by and revelatory of emotion, the notion of expression as artistic creation requires no conceptual tie between expression and emotions, feelings, or moods—at least the ordinary sorts of emotions experienced outside art.

Assume the common-sense notion of expression as conceptually tied to emotions—and stipulate that 'emotion' encompasses a whole range of affective phenomena, including emotions proper, feelings, moods, and the like. The differences between these affective phenomena are important but not well understood, and we should not allow our conception of expression to be biased toward any one.

The history of writing about notions of expression tied to emotion follows an interesting trajectory that has shaped contemporary thinking.

From the Renaissance until the eighteenth century, theorists focused on the depiction of figures expressing emotional states via the arrangement of their limbs and the configurations of their faces—what Leonardo called the 'air of faces'. This is

figure expression: an expression that is wholly attributable to a depicted person or persons.

Leonardo remarks that a 'figure is most praiseworthy which best expresses through its actions the passions of its mind' and that any figure inexpressive in this sense is 'twice dead, inasmuch as it is dead because it is a depiction, and dead yet again in not exhibiting either motion of the mind or of the body' (1989: 144). This implies, plausibly enough, that persons have minds and are capable of action.

The most influential systematic treatment of figure expression along these lines is Charles Le Brun's catalogue of human facial expressions and the ways of drawing them that give the impression of faces in movement rather than fixed grimaces (Le Brun 2000; Montagu 1994). In this tradition, figure expression is taken to be an instrument of narrative depiction, especially history painting. Since narrative is the representation of action, and action is movement done for a reason, the point of a figure's expression is to reveal at a glance the springs of its action (Ross 1984). *Fatherly Discipline* is a family drama whose actors wear expressions that economically convey what they feel, what they want, and what they are trying to do.

Although Le Brun's enterprise lives on in the atlases of facial expression consulted by amateur painters, theorists began to lose interest in figure expression by the nineteenth century, when they turned attention to another expressive phenomenon.

The whole of a depicted scene may express an emotion that is expressed by no figures in the scene. An image of moorland may be gloomy, a sunrise hopeful, and craggy rocks surly. Call this

scene expression: an expression that is attributable at least in part to a depicted scene and is not wholly attributable to any depicted persons.

The phenomenon of scene expression was acknowledged by some writers of the early period (e.g. Poussin 1958; Testelin 2000), but only in the nineteenth century did it receive the kind of comprehensive and systematic treatment given to figure expression. By the twentieth century, figure expression had been deeply discounted in favour of scene expression, which nicely harmonizes with the expression theory of art. For example, Matisse insisted that expression lies not 'in passions glowing in a human face or manifested by violent movement. The entire arrangement of my picture is expressive' (1992: 73). His *Red Studio* is a striking example.

The key mechanism of scene expression was widely held to be colour. The eighteenth-century theorist Jonathan Richardson advised that

> the Colouring of a Picture must be varied according to the Subject, the Time, and the Place. If the Subject be Grave, Melancholy, or Terrible, the General Tinct of the Colouring must incline to Brown, Black, or Red, and Gloomy; but be Gay, and Pleasant in Subjects of Joy and Triumph. (Quoted in Montagu 1994: 99)

Later accounts of scene expression attempted to schematize the expressiveness of colours, often by analogy with the expressive properties of musical harmonies (Gage 1993: 227–46).

Modes of pictorial expression

The classic sources in the theory of expression each focus upon one mode of expression, but neither may be overlooked by a philosophy of pictorial expression. This stricture is doubly important because most recent philosophical accounts of expression in the arts concern pure music (without lyrics), in which cases of figure expression are freakish exceptions. A good antidote to a history of selective attention is to keep in mind a range of cases.

One might think that there is no need to distinguish between scene and figure expression because the two always correspond. This is not so. The shipwrecked, starving figures aboard Delacroix's *Raft of the Medusa* express despair; the roiling sea in which they are set adrift expresses dumb, haughty malignance; and the tiny ship on the horizon that might signify safe harbour instead expresses blind indifference. What is expressed by the depicted figures and by the depicted scene fails to correspond. Indeed, the story the picture tells requires us to note the failure, much as the story in *Fatherly Discipline* requires us to see how the three depicted figures are so painfully out of step.

This is not to rule out correspondence. The seascape in Munch's *Scream* (Fig. 9) exactly echoes what is expressed on the face of its protagonist. Maybe the look of the seascape is a projection of the

Fig. 9. *Left*, Edvard Munch, *The Scream*, 1893; *middle*, principal figure excised; *right*, scene excised.

protagonist's anguish. If so, the seascape's look is a case of figure expression. However, it is just as likely that the protagonist's mental state is a response to an anguished, alienating world. In this drawing, figure and scene expression are unified: one enhances but does not depend on the other.

Some cases might encourage the idea that figure expression consists in the representation of expressive behaviours, while scene expression has only to do with a picture's non-representational or formal features. This idea is propounded in the classic sources, in which expression is first viewed as the representation of expressive faces and later comes to be viewed as the non-representational evocation of emotion. The idea pits representation and expression against each other by reducing figure expression to representation and leaving scene expression as the sole mode of expression proper.

On the contrary, a poignant panel from Art Spiegelman's *Maus* (Fig. 10) expresses a sense of pervasive foreboding as much by how it depicts the world (as a crossroads that is a swastika) as through its formal features. Here scene expression is a matter of representation. Likewise, figure expression can leverage formal resources. The violently fractured planes of Picasso's *Weeping Head* contribute to the figure's expressiveness.

One might also suppose that only figure expression serves a narrative purpose or requires a narrative context. What is expressed by the central figure in Rembrandt's painting of the denial of Christ by Peter unlocks the nuances of the story, and familiarity with the story is needed to perceive what the figure expresses. In limiting cases, such as *Fatherly Discipline*, the narrative comprises nothing but what the figures express. Appreciation of what each figure expresses is achieved only by setting it in the context of what the other figures express, and appreciation of the story lies wholly in seeing what the figures express.

Similar dynamics are at work in some cases of scene expression, however. The story of the *Medusa* is told in part through what the distant ship and the sea express. What the scene depicted in the panel from *Maus* expresses depends on its place in a story that it also

Fig. 10. Art Spiegelman, Panel from *Maus I: A Survivor's Tale/My Father Bleeds History.* Copyright © 1973, 1980, 1981, 1982, 1984, 1985, 1986 by Art Spiegelman. Used by permission of Pantheon Books, a division of Random House Inc., and Penguin Books Ltd.

helps to tell. Scene expression may advance a narrative purpose or depend upon a narrative framework.

Figure expression and scene expression are achieved depictively. The claim is not that expression is depiction. Rather, a picture may express an emotion by depicting a figure or scene as expressing the emotion. Thus figure and scene expressions are seen in pictures.

Not every emotion a picture expresses is seen as expressed by something depicted. Non-representational paintings, such as Jackson Pollock's drip paintings, are expressive. They are expressive in the way Mondrian has in mind when he complains that curves are too emotional—the trouble is with the curves themselves, not with anything that they depict. The same phenomenon is at work in representational images. A picture, no matter what its depictive content, may express anger or frustration or some other emotion because it is composed of clashing red and green triangles. Call this

design expression: an expression that is wholly attributable to a picture's design or surface and not to any figure or scene it depicts.

Design expression is a third mode of pictorial expression in addition to figure expression and scene expression. Figure and scene expressions are depicted expressions; design expressions are not.

Obviously, a picture's design expression may contribute to or undermine what it expresses mimetically. The coiled lines used to render the faces and hands of father and child in Daumier's drawing express a tension and anxiety that amplifies the expressions worn by the figures themselves. The clashing navy blue and tangerine orange used to render the seascape in *The Scream* enhance what that scene expresses.

The Missing Person Problem

We evaluate pictures for the expressiveness of their designs or of the figures or scenes they depict. Since evaluations of pictures as sad need not track evaluations of experiences of actual persons as sad, we must address the puzzle of mimesis for expression. But another problem takes priority. Different solutions to it make for different theories of pictorial expression.

About to kiss the frog, the princess grimaces. The frog sees the configuration of the princess's face but, being a frog, cannot see it as a grimace. The moral of the story is that expressions are more than mere physical configurations. They are connected, somehow, to emotions. According to the

connection condition: an expression is not merely a physical configuration; it is a physical configuration connected to an emotion.

The condition additionally suggests that to see an expression as an expression is to see a physical configuration as connected to an emotion. This is what the frog cannot do.

What is the connection? Emotions are mental states that normally commence in a thinker's appraisal of her environment and terminate in some behaviour, frequently one that enables her to cope with her environment, either by modifying it or by modifying herself. So a plausible idea is that expressions are physical configurations that outwardly manifest and indicate thinkers' emotional states. Expression is one part of emotion. Zombies cannot smile because they are incapable of happiness. Zombies can turn up their lips, but that is not smiling.

The conception of expression as part of emotion applies quite smoothly to figure expression. Some of Bruegel's peasants are depicted as smiling: the configurations of their faces are smiles in the sense that they are part of their happiness. By depicting them as smiling, Bruegel represents the peasants as happy. To see them as smiling is to see them as revealing, by the way they arrange their faces, how they feel.

The problem is that in scene expression, by definition, no person is depicted as the bearer of the emotion expressed. Scene expression raises a missing person problem. Unless there can be expression in the absence of a being to whom the expressed emotion is attributable, then either there is no scene expression or the being in question is one not depicted.

Three strategies are available: (1) deny that there is scene expression in pictures, (2) attribute the emotion that is putatively expressed by a scene to some person who is *not depicted*, or (3) allow that expression of emotion does not require that there be anyone to whom the emotion expressed is attributable. The examples we have already considered make it clear that (1) is a last resort.

If Zombies cannot Smile

Suppose that (2) is true, and so an emotion expressed by a depicted scene is to be attributed to a person who is not depicted. Who is that person? Here are three answers: the picture's maker, an implied persona within the depicted world, and the picture's spectator. Unless we have good reason to accept one of these answers, we should prefer (3) to (2).

Personalism: creator as expressor

One way to solve the missing person problem is to pin scene expression on the picture-maker: it is this person whose emotions get expressed in a picture. Some replace the actual picture-maker with an implied or hypothetical picture-maker whose characteristics are determined by the best rational reconstruction of the work's creation. Let the 'creator' of a work be either the person who actually made it or a hypothetical person whose characteristics best explain its making. The proposal is that we should attribute the emotions expressed in a scene to the picture's creator.

If van Gogh's *Wheatfield with Crows* is not expressive, then what is? The sky blazes so blue that it is almost black, while the grain, intensely yellow, pushes vigorously against the horizon. Overhanging this determined, even forced, joy is a flock of crows, expressing foreboding. Yet no person in this scene is depicted as having any of these emotions. According to one version of personalism, we are to understand the picture as expressing van Gogh's emotions (where 'van Gogh' may name a hypothetical person rather than the actual maker of the picture). He externalizes his emotions by painting a scene expressing them.

This proposal echoes a widely accepted romantic conception of creative action—one on which van Gogh headlines as a paradigm creator. On this conception, the creator of a picture is someone who feels something, can express it only by making a picture, and the picture she makes is an expression of what she feels.

It should be obvious that creator expression is a species of natural expression. Natural expressions are expressions of emotion in 'real life' contexts—Jimmy Carter's smiling, Arnold Schwartzenegger's teeth gritting, and Pierre Trudeau's giving the sign of the fig. Some of these are stereotyped or conventionalized gestures, such as smiles and snarls. Others are *sui generis*, not determined either by innate psycho-physiological mechanisms or conventions for signalling emotions. Examples include expressing anger by keying a car, expressing joy by sliding down a banister, and expressing sadness by sitting alone on a beach.

If so inclined, and if supplied with brush, paint, and canvas, I might mark the surface of a painting with riotously discordant colours and shapes. The resulting design is a *sui generis* expression of anger, which is attributable to me, just as my snarling and car-keying are expressions of anger attributable to me. What goes for design expression also goes for scene expression, since expression may tap the resources of depiction as well as those of language and bodily movement. Feeling a kind of dark joy tinged with foreboding, van Gogh paints a picture of crows descending from a blue-black sky over intensely yellow wheat. The scene expresses an emotion that is van Gogh's, not the landscape's, though it is through the look of the landscape that he betrays his emotion.

The proposal is not far-fetched. Pictures are regularly used in clinical settings to diagnose the emotional state of those who are unable to articulate difficult emotions. The disturbed child draws pictures of figures or inanimate scenes expressing his painful emotions. Similarly, a creator may draw to expose and articulate his feelings about his life or the world.

Granting these points, there are problems with attributing all expressed emotions to a creator. The states of mind involved in creative activity may conflict with the emotions a picture expresses, so that it is impossible to attribute both to one and the same creator. Joshua Reynolds presumably wrote from experience that,

a Painter, whatever he may feel, will not be able to express it on canvas, without having recourse to a recollection of those principles by which that passion is expressed; the mind thus occupied, is not likely at the same time to be possessed with the passion which he is representing, an image may be ludicrous, and in its first conception makes the Painter laugh as well as the Spectator; but the difficulty of his art makes the Painter, in the course of his work, equally grave and serious, whether he is employed on the most ludicrous, or the most solemn subjects. (Quoted in Montagu 1994: 6)

As Wollheim puts it, pictorial expression is 'controlled, and boosted, by reflection upon, and by recollection of, the emotion' (1987: 87). Control of and reflection upon an emotion for the purpose of depicting a scene is sometimes incompatible with feeling the emotion. Feeling terrified interferes with the calm and thoughtful retrieval of the expression of fear needed for painting a picture whose design or scene expresses fear.

Reynolds and Wollheim are raising a question about method. The conditions needed for emotions to arise and thus be expressed are sometimes, if not always, defeated by the conditions needed for creativity. In such cases, the emotion that a picture's design or scene expresses may not be the emotion we have best reason to attribute to its creator.

While doodling, I draw a happy face. The happy face expresses happiness—it is nowadays the archetypal expression of happiness. Yet doodling is as absent-hearted as it is absent-minded. Thus we can generalize from design and scene expression to figure expression: there is no necessary tie between what a figure expresses and what a creator feels.

An obvious reply is that the case of the happy face is not pertinent. We properly attribute to creators nuanced emotions that can find expression *only* in pictures. Personalism applies to *Fatherly Discipline*, not the happy face.

However, the doodle also teaches us that a design, scene, or figure may express an emotion in order to serve a creative purpose that does not originate with that emotion, or any emotion. The purpose of my doodle may be to pass the time in sweet mindlessness. Or perhaps boredom impels me to doodle a hundred happy faces: the faces express happiness, but my making them betrays only boredom. So when a picture is generated from an emotion of its creator, there is no reason to suppose it must have a design or depict a scene or figures expressing the very same emotion. (The point does not hinge on identifying the creator of *Hundred Happy Faces* with its flesh-and-blood maker. If it is evidently a doodle and not pop art, we have good reason to attribute boredom to its hypothetical maker too.)

Likewise, we may grant that the frustration expressed in *Fatherly Discipline* could be Daumier's. But equally the depicted father expressing frustration might serve to express an emotion of Daumier's other than frustration—outrage, perhaps, at something he saw or knew about. More plausibly, Daumier's purpose is to tell a story that provokes thought about the emotional dynamics of situations like the one he depicts. Telling a story does not require having the emotions that characters in the story have or express.

The same goes for scene expression—the cold hatred and foreboding expressed by the scene in the panel from *Maus*, for example. It makes little sense to say that the scene expresses Spiegelman's emotion, though many emotions are likely to have come into play in his conception of the panel. Rather, the scene serves a narrative end—in an especially compelling way. If scene expression is independent of creative emotion, then what is it for the picture to express foreboding? The answer is not that the scene feels foreboding, for scenes feel nothing.

None of this controverts the view that people do sometimes make pictures that express their emotions, especially complex and nuanced emotions that are not effectively expressible in other media. According to what one might call the romantic conception of the artist, this is exactly what artists should strive to do. Moreover, it is perfectly legitimate to attempt a theory of this kind of expression and the romantic conception of artistic creation (e.g. Robinson 2005). Nevertheless, such a theory does not explain what it is to attribute an expression to a pictorial design, a depicted figure, or a depicted scene. What a picture expresses may not be what the creator feels.

The missing person problem remains unsolved for scene expression: what is it for a depicted scene to express an emotion attributable neither to the scene nor to the picture's creator?

Hypothetical personalism

There are symmetrical and asymmetrical solutions to the missing person problem for scene expression. According to asymmetrical solutions, scene expression is the expression of a person outside the picture (e.g. its creator), whereas figure expression is the expression of a person in the world of the picture. On symmetrical solutions, the emotion a scene expresses is to be attributed to a person who is in the world of the picture but is not depicted. Whereas the vehicle for the expression of the emotion of a depicted figure is usually the depicted figure's body, the vehicle for the expression of the emotion of an undepicted person in the world of the picture is the arrangement of the inanimate depicted scene. The emotion expressed by a scene is to be attributed to a 'hypothetical persona' (Vermazen 1986; Robinson 1994; Levinson 1996*a*).

The hypothetical persona is not a creator: he is not someone who expresses his emotion by *depicting* the scene. He expresses his emotion through a scene much as an actual person might adjust her face to express her emotion. Your smile expresses your happiness; the resplendent lightness of the city in Turner's *Heidelberg Sunset* is an unusual yet apt expression of the happiness not of Turner but of a hypothetical persona. It is as if the scene is sensitive to, tuned into, arranging itself to reveal, the hypothetical persona's emotional state. He does not express his emotion by *painting* a sunset; he expresses his emotion through the sunset itself.

We have seen that attributions of expressed emotions to a picture's *creator* run afoul of conflicting attributions that pick up on facts about the creative process. The hypothetical persona version of personalism is immune to this conflict, for the hypothetical persona is not a creator, and so does not have the conflicting properties. A study of the making of *Heidelberg Sunset* may uncover facts showing that Turner could not have been expressing his happiness by making a picture of a happy-looking scene. No matter. These facts are consistent with the picture's hypothetical persona being happy and revealing her happiness through the brilliantly illuminated city.

There is no reason to deny that emotions expressed by a depicted scene may be attributed to a hypothetical persona. After all, what fact about a hypothetical persona could block such an attribution? The only facts to which the attributions commit us are that the persona has the attributed emotion and that she is a fiction.

This is as much a weakness of the view as its strength, however, if attributions of emotions to hypothetical personas are trivial. They are trivial if they are made only in order to conform to the rule that expressed emotions must be attributed to persons—if there is no *additional* fact about scene expression or our experience of it that is explained by the attribution of expressed emotions to hypothetical personas.

Contrast scene expression with musical expression and figure expression. Much pure music expresses a sequence of emotions, and understanding the music requires that some sense be made of the sequence. We ask why those emotions are expressed in that order and with those musical materials; we are puzzled when some expressive stretch of music seems not to be integrated into the sequence; and we are disappointed should we learn that integration is impossible. Attributing each emotion in the sequence to a musical persona helps the task of integration by enabling us to hear the sequence as a narrative. The sequence from anger to despair to wise resignation, for example, makes sense as part of the history of a person.

By contrast, emotions expressed by depicted scenes are not sequential and are rarely if ever narratives (though they may help tell stories about depicted figures). The hypothetical persona in painting does not afford access to the rich tools of narrative explanation that are the key contribution of the hypothetical persona in pure music.

One benefit of attributing emotions expressed by figures to the figures depicted is that it helps us to make sense of their actions within a narrative context. What is expressed by the figures in *Fatherly Discipline* makes sense of the scenario it depicts. Viewing it as an interpersonal drama, we come to see, for instance, that the mother's shocked and sad reaction to the father's frustrated anger is tinged with disappointment.

Anything we gain by attributing figure expressions to depicted figures dissipates as the figures lose determinacy. The figures in *Fatherly Discipline* are relatively determinate, but figure expression does not require high levels of determinacy. The happy face depicts a smiling person and thereby depicts it as looking happy, but Mr or Ms H. Face is depicted as having no properties in addition to his or her looking happy and the very few properties in virtue of which that look is conveyed. No fact—about a narrative, for instance—explains the happy face picture's expressing Happy's feeling happy that does not just explain its simply depicting a look of happiness.

Scene expression is more like the happy face than *Fatherly Discipline*. If a feeling of foreboding is attributed to a hypothetical persona whose emotional state is expressed in the panel from *Maus*, that persona is highly indeterminate. It has that emotion and some properties that are needed to account for its expressing its emotional state in the scene as it is depicted. There is no fact that explains the picture's expressing the emotional state of the hypothetical persona unless it equally explains how the picture simply looks foreboding.

None of these observations refute hypothetical personalism. They simply narrow the gap, in cases of scene expression, between seeing an expression as expression of an emotion attributed to some person and seeing it non-personally, as a physical configuration that is an appropriate vehicle for indicating an emotion. The facts about the look of a depicted scene to which we are attuned when an expressed emotion is attributed to a non-depicted persona are frequently just those to which we are attuned when we see the scene as expressing an unattributed emotion.

Arousalism

The mirror image of personalism is arousalism. Both views presume that if an emotion expressed cannot be attributed to a person depicted, then it must be attributed to a person not depicted;

but arousalism locates the person in question in front of, not behind, the picture. The point is not just that pictures *do* arouse emotional responses in those who look at them, nor is it that they arouse responses to what they express. Nobody denies that the scene depicted in the panel from *Maus* (Fig. 10) elicits from the book's reader a feeling of sinking dread. Arousalism asserts that the scene's (or design's or figure's) expressing what it does is constituted at least in part by its arousing a response from the reader. Arousal is not a side-effect of expression; it is part of expression. The spectator fills the missing person's shoes.

As a point of clarification, arousalism states the conditions under which expression occurs; it does not attempt to characterize the value of expression. Perhaps the expressiveness of a picture is a merit only when it moves the viewer emotionally, but this is no reason to endorse arousalism. After all, the meritorious is not always the required. Let us postpone this matter until the end of the chapter.

A second point of clarification is needed to distinguish recent upgrades of arousalism from legacy arousalism. Alberti wrote that 'it happens in nature that nothing more than herself is found capable of things like herself: we weep with the weeping, laugh with the laughing, and grieve with the grieving. These movements of the soul are made known by movements of the body' (1966: 77). For Alberti, pictorial expression, like natural expression, involves emotional contagion. Giovanni Lomazzo added in 1584 that a person looking at a picture will come to 'desire a beautiful woman for his wife, when he sees her painted naked . . . to have an appetite when he sees the eating of dainties; to fall asleep at the sight of a sweet-sleeping picture; to be moved and wax furious when he beholds a battle most lively described' (quoted in Montagu 1994: 64).

Lomazzo's claim is obviously preposterous. Emotions alert perceivers to certain features of their environment and prepare them to act appropriately, but the picture-viewer's emotional state does not normally cause, dispose, or even motivate her to act accordingly. Fight and flight are the responses associated with fear, but visitors to the National Gallery neither turn on their heels nor break out their karate moves at the sight of pictures of battles.

Also mistaken is Alberti's more sensible idea that viewers both feel and express the emotion that a picture expresses. The spectator need not express what he feels—however soft his heart, he may remain dry-eyed. More importantly, the emotional state of the spectator need not be, and often should not be, the same as the one expressed by the picture. The scene in the panel from *Maus* expresses sinking dread, but we should and do react with pity and indignation. The picture's expression is successful because our reaction is appropriate, not because it mirrors what is expressed. If it provokes chuckles in normal people, its expression is a failure.

Viable versions of arousalism must therefore accommodate two facts. First, the arousal of an emotion in a picture's viewer need not involve the behaviours, including expressive ones, that are characteristic of the emotion. Second, the emotion aroused need not be the very one that the picture expresses: it need only be an emotion appropriately aroused in response to what the picture expresses.

Derek Matravers proposes that a work expresses an emotion only if, for a qualified perceiver viewing it in the right circumstances, the work arouses in the perceiver a feeling which would be an appropriate reaction to the expression of the very same emotion by a person (1998: 146). Sometimes the appropriate response to an expression is to have the very emotion expressed. If the appropriate response to a person's expression of joy is to share in it, then the appropriate response to a picture expressive of joy is to feel joy. Sometimes the appropriate response to the expression of an emotion is to feel a different emotion. If pity is the appropriate response to a person's expression of sadness, then pity is the appropriate response to a picture expressing sadness.

Arousalism solves the missing person problem: for every expression attributed to a scene or design we are to attribute an appropriate responsive emotion to the picture's viewer. It also derives substantial plausibility from the fact that pictures do arouse emotions—and so are highly valued. Should we believe it, though?

The best argument for arousalism trades on the connection condition. An expression is no mere physical configuration, and this suggests that there is more to seeing an expression as an expression than seeing a physical configuration. Arousalism explains this datum. What bridges the gap from merely seeing a physical configuration to seeing it as an expression of a particular emotion is the viewer's emotional arousal, which inflects her visual experience of the physical configuration with an emotional component. The proposition that expression is partly constituted by arousal parses the distinction between expressions and mere physical arrangements in a way that explains how seeing the former does not collapse into seeing the latter.

This argument requires more than arousalism is able to deliver, however. Emotional arousal bridges the gap between seeing an expression as a mere physical arrangement and seeing it as an expression only if emotions expressed correlate in a relatively tidy way with emotions appropriately aroused. The correlation need not amount to identity; it is sufficient if emotions appropriately aroused track emotions expressed—that is, if A is appropriately aroused only in response to B, C only to D, E only to F, and so on.

As a matter of fact, though, the same emotion is appropriately aroused in response to any number of expressed emotions. Sadness is an appropriate response to the grief of the woman depicted in Picasso's *Weeping Head*, to the incontinent fury expressed by the principal actor in *Fatherly Discipline*, to the dread expressed in the panel from *Maus*, and to the indifference of the distant ship in the *Raft of the Medusa*. The same emotion, when it is appropriately aroused in response to different expressions, cannot comprise seeing the expressions, as long as they are seen as different from one another.

One might reply that this objection sets the bar too high for arousalism. The aroused feeling is required only in order to inject an affective element into seeing an expression, thereby animating the sight of the mere physical configuration. It is the physical configuration itself that gives the experience sufficiently fine-grained content, so that one sees that expression rather than another. The viewer's emotional contribution to expression is generic.

The reply is costly. Suppose I see one scene as having a certain look, which is converted to a look of fear by the addition of a dash of generic affect, and suppose I see another scene as having another look, which is converted to a look of dread by the addition of a dash of generic affect. What is lost in the content of my seeing if the spice is withheld? Why not say that the first look is a look of fear and the second a look of dread? Putting the point another way, it is much harder than one would expect for expression to fail. The scene in the panel from *Maus* elicits chuckles? No matter, for the look of the scene is one of dread, and it does arouse *some* emotional response, so it succeeds in expressing dread. The requirement that the emotion aroused be appropriate to that expressed explains nothing. The emotion aroused is phenomenological window-dressing.

Biting the bullet, the arousalist may insist that the looks are not expressions until the affective component is added: seeing a physical configuration associated with an expression of fear is not seeing it as an expression of fear until the experience gets inflected by some emotional arousal.

Insisting on this solves the missing person problem in the case of scene expression. It also explains what is involved in seeing an expression as an expression rather than a mere physical arrangement. By the same token, however, anyone who denies that the missing person problem is a problem in the first place may happily assume two tasks. One is to give an account of expression as more than a mere physical configuration. Flowing from this is a second task: namely, to pin-point what is present in seeing an expression as an expression and absent in seeing a mere physical configuration.

If Dogs can Smile

Personalism and arousalism endeavour to solve the missing person problem for scene expression while assuming that there can be no expression unless there is some person to whom the emotion expressed is attributable. Once this assumption is dropped, one difference between figure expression and scene expression loses its grip on us. We need no longer worry that in one case some person is depicted as having the emotion expressed whereas in the other case nobody is so depicted. Freed from this worry, we may adopt an impersonal theory of pictorial expression roughly modelled on contour theories of musical and natural expression (Stephen Davies 1980; Kivy 1989). On these theories, a dog can smile when it is not happy (and so can zombies).

Expression and resemblance

Robust contour theories of expression conjoin two claims. The first is that a depicted figure or scene expresses an emotion by wearing an expression-look associated with that emotion. This claim states what it is for a figure or scene to express: it has an expression-look. The second claim states what determines the connection between the expression-look and an emotion. A figure or scene looks to express an emotion if it looks like a natural ('real life') expression of the same emotion. On the

robust contour theory of pictorial expression: a pictorial design, a depicted figure, or a depicted scene expresses an emotion, E, if and only if (1) it is an expression-look that (2) resembles a natural expression-look of E.

In the textbook example, to say that a Saint Bernard dog expresses sadness is to say that she wears the look of sadness. She wears the look of sadness (rather than puzzlement or congeniality) because she looks like a sad human. Similarly, a depicted figure or scene looks sad because it looks like a sad human seen face to face. The view must address several problems.

First is the puzzle of mimesis. Junior expresses frustration: he looks frustrated. Depicted Junior expresses frustration only because he looks like Junior looks. We should predict that any evaluation of the picture for its depicting Junior's frustrated expression applies as well to seeing Junior's expression of frustration face to face. None the less, predictions like this are typically wrong.

Note that personalism and arousalism do not face this problem. Personalism, for example, claims that expressions are components of and reveal emotions. Some expressions are fast, automatic, and stereotyped, such as the look of anger. Others are conventional, such as the utterance 'I'm furious'. Yet others are *sui generis*, such as keying an enemy's car out of anger. Many pictorial expressions— all scene and design expressions—are either *sui generis* or else governed by specifically pictorial conventions. In each case, expression clearly conforms to the connection condition. In each case, too, seeing what a depicted figure, creator, or hypothetical persona expresses need be nothing like seeing face to face a person expressing the same emotion.

Another difficulty concerns the plausibility of the claim that every expression-look of a figure, scene, or design resembles some natural expression-look of a person. What is the resemblance between the look of the sea in the *Raft of the Medusa* and a person who looks haughtily malignant? What is the resemblance between the coiled lines in the design of *Fatherly Discipline* and a person who looks frustrated to his wits' end? Or between a 'brown Tinct' and a person who looks grave? These questions do have answers, of course, since everything resembles everything else in some respect. Nevertheless, it is hard to see how the answers will pick out resemblances that are independent of, and so capable of determining, what emotion is expressed.

Both objections target the second claim endorsed in robust contour theories—the resemblance claim. Suppose we relinquish this claim (Goodman 1976). Standing in contrast to the robust contour theory is a

minimal contour theory of pictorial expression: a pictorial design, a depicted figure, or a depicted scene expresses E if and only if it is an expression-look of E.

Given up is the claim that what makes the pictorial expression-look an expression-look of E (and not of something else) is a resemblance between the picture or something it depicts and a natural expression-look of E.

The minimal contour theory absolves us from hunting for resemblances that determine what looks express. It also solves the puzzle of expressive mimesis. The expression-look of E in a picture need not resemble the expression-look of E in some person seen face to face.

Can the contour theory survive the amputation of the resemblance claim? What is left of the minimal theory tells us that expression is impersonal—we cannot infer from something's expressing E that it or anything feels E. Does this satisfy the connection condition, according to which an expression is a physical configuration connected to an emotion? In the robust contour theory, the resemblance claim meets the connection condition, but that claim has been given up.

Assume, plausibly, that the connection condition applies to all three modes of pictorial expression. The contour theory must be built up so as to satisfy the condition. Construction materials can be scrounged from a theory of natural expression.

Natural expression

Expression-looks are familiar in ordinary, extra-pictorial contexts. Jimmy's smile looks to express happiness, Julia's lipped lick looks to express gustatory delight, George's scratch of the head looks to express bewilderment, and Joe's end-zone dance looks to express joy. Something can be learned from these natural expression-looks about their pictorial kin, not only in figure expression but in scene and design expression too.

One obvious lesson is that attributing an expression-look to a person does not require attributing an emotion to the person. Sometimes we describe a person as 'happy-looking', and we do not mean to imply that we take the person to *be* happy. My being impressed by your cheerful demeanour following the crash of your cherished automobile requires that I not believe you to be cheerful: I am describing your look, not your emotional state, and I realize that your look conceals your true emotional state.

So expression-looks are not always emotion-indicators. A smile indicates that the smiler is happy only when it is caused by her happiness. It fails to indicate happiness when it is worn for purposes of pretence or deception. Furthermore, not every visible behaviour caused by an emotional state is an expression-look. The sleepless-ness induced by a triumph is not an expression of one's pride in the triumph. One need not look as one feels or feel as one looks.

Expression-looks are not the same as emotion-inducers either. Although a smile typically provokes an emotional response on the part of suitably primed onlookers, it remains an expression-look even as members of the company remain unmoved. Furthermore, not every visible behaviour that induces an emotional response is an expression-look. The dealer's declaring the gaming table closed is no expression of despair (or any other emotion), though it may induce despair on the part of the day's unlucky players. No state of emotional arousal can be inferred merely from the occurrence of an expression-look, and no expression-look can be inferred merely from a state of arousal.

What, then, is an expression-look? An expression-look is a physical configuration that has the function, in the circumstances, of indicating an emotion. This can be plugged into a

contour theory of natural expression: a physical configuration expresses E if and only if (1) it is an expression-look that (2) has the function, in the circumstances, of indicating E.

The physical configuration could be a movement, a gesture, an utterance, or some event. The contour theory also suggests an account of what it is to see an expression as an expression. To see a physical configuration as an expression is to see it as something that has the function, in the circumstances, of indicating an emotion—as something that, as it were, should indicate the emotion.

This version of the contour theory derails the train of thought that leads to the missing person problem. Some expression-looks indicate emotions, but all that is required for a physical configuration to be an expression of an emotion is that it be an expression-look with the function of indicating that emotion. Zombies can smile, though they are incapable of feeling happiness, so long as they can wear looks that have the function of indicating happiness. A natural expression of an emotion is an appearance that need not be part of, or even caused by, the emotion. It is not essentially personal.

And yet the contour theory of natural expression meets the connection condition. An expression is more than a physical configuration: it is a physical configuration that is connected to an emotion by having the function of indicating the emotion. Someone may smack their lips, but their lip smacking is not an expression of delight unless it has the function in the circumstances of indicating delight. Thus to see an expression as an expression, and not merely as a physical configuration, is at least to see it as something designed to indicate the emotion.

Mechanisms of expression

Why does a licked lip have the function of indicating delight? Why does the thrust of a fist have the function of indicating angry contempt? Why does the end-zone dance have the function of expressing joy? How can we say that the Saint Bernard's face looks sad, when it looks that way no matter how the dog feels? These questions suggest two more general questions about the contour theory of natural expression.

First, what is it for a physical arrangement to have the function of indicating an emotion? Many answers to this question will do, and the theory implies no one of them. Here are the rough outlines of one answer (see Dretske 1981, 1988; cf. Fodor 1990). It might be the right answer, or it might be a good model for the right answer.

Smoke indicates fire, and measles indicate an infection of *Morbillivirus*. In each of these cases the indicator state carries information about an indicated state: given the indicator's state, the conditional probability of the indicated state is one in one. The position of a speedometer needle also indicates something—for example, that the vehicle is moving at 50 kilometres per hour. Normally it does this by carrying information about the speed of the vehicle. However, the needle can fail to carry information about the speed of the vehicle—it may be broken or subject to some kind of interference. Even then it has the function of indicating the speed of the vehicle because it is part of a system designed to carry information about vehicle speed.

Natural expression-looks frequently carry information about emotions. If your happiness causes you to smile, your smile carries the information that you are happy. However, feeling unhappy, you might smile none the less. By the same token, your happiness might cause you to buy a round of drinks, so that your buying the drinks carries the information that you are happy, but it is not an expression of happiness. Expression-looks are more like speedometer needles than measles. The smile is part of a mechanism designed (in fact, evolved) to carry information about emotions. It has the function of indicating happiness. Buying drinks is not an expression of happiness, because it does not have the function in the circumstances of indicating happiness.

This leads to a second, separate question, about the mechanisms by means of which any given physical configuration has the function of indicating a given emotion.

Many mechanisms can be used to measure an automobile's speed. The most common counts the rotations of a cog attached to a wheel's hub. Coming soon is one which uses GPS to measure changes in map location over time, hence speed. Facts about these mechanisms determine what each state of the speedometer dial has the function of indicating. What mechanisms determine that some physical configurations have the function of indicating some emotions? After all, not any physical configuration may express any emotion in given circumstances. Romantic disappointment is associated (in some circles) with the consumption of chocolate, but the consumption of chocolate is not an expression of romantic sadness. Why not?

There are well-known general constraints on what states can have the function of indicating other states. For example, indicator states may be no less fine-grained than indicated states—a typical analog wall clock cannot have the function of indicating milliseconds. There must also be some sufficiently reliable correlation between indicator and indicated states—dice rolls cannot have the function of indicating student test performances. The contour theory will incorporate any constraints imposed by the best theory of indication.

It is not obvious, though, that there are any *special* constraints on what looks can have the function of indicating what emotions. This is intuitively hard to swallow. Smiles and pirouettes seem especially well fitted to indicating happiness, and the extruded tongue and gag gesture to indicating disgust. In truth, there is nothing about smiles that fits them to have the function of indicating happiness. The smile could have had the function of indicating disgust, and the extruded tongue that of indicating happiness. Links between looks and emotions are contingent and not specially constrained.

The psychologist Paul Ekman has identified several classes of mechanisms of natural expression. Some physiological processes have the function of indicating emotions—blushing betrays embarrassment—though not all physiological effects function to indicate their causes—the high adrenalin levels caused by fear are not expressions of it. A similar class of mechanisms make use of body motion and position, content of utterance, and vocal tone (Ekman, Friesen, and Ellsworth 1982: III).

No facial configuration or gesture has the function of indicating embarrassment by itself, but the presence of an embarrassing situation helps to determine that a look has the function in the circumstances of indicating embarrassment. Mechanisms of 'referential expression' are crucially dependent on context.

An example is the 'miserable smile' commonly seen in such places as dentists' offices (Ekman 1984: 323). The miserable smile and the smile reserved for viewing babies each have the function of indicating different emotions in different circumstances. Relevant contextual factors include display rules, conventions, norms, and habits that govern who can express what, when, how, and to whom. In beauty contests, for example, winners may cry, but losers must smile (Ekman 1980: 87). Knowledge of which expressions are licensed and which are proscribed in a given situation helps determine what emotion a look has the function of indicating. Finally, context enters in cases of secondary expression, where one expression depends on another—where, for example, a look's having the function of indicating anger depends on its also having the function of indicating embarrassment—as in certain blushes.

Some mechanisms designed to indicate emotions are innate, but many are conventional, hence social. The social *need not* be conventional, however. Someone may express her joy by sliding down the banister and turning a pirouette at the bottom, but there is no convention or innate disposition to ride banisters and pirouette when joyous. The mechanisms underlying *sui generis* expressions like this one are not well understood. They share much in common with metaphorical and ironic language. Some utterances have the function, in given circumstances, of indicating irony, and some *sui generis* movements and gestures have the function, in given circumstances, of indicating joy.

It is disappointing when we know the least about what is most interesting. Nevertheless, ignorance about the mechanisms of expression is no reason to reject the contour theory. The theory says what it is to be an expression of an emotion: a physical configuration expresses E if and only if it is a look that has the function in the circumstances of indicating E. This is true even if we do not know what mechanisms underlie the look's having that indicating function rather than another, or none at all.

It is crucial to distinguish two tasks. One is to say what it is for a physical configuration to express a particular emotion. Success in this task satisfies the emotional connection condition. A separate task is to identify mechanisms of expression. The robust contour theory of pictorial expression attempts both tasks by invoking resemblance to accomplish the second. The minimal contour theory of pictorial expression does not even acknowledge the second.

Pictorial Expression

The contour theory of natural expression inspires a

contour theory of pictorial expression: the physical configuration of a picture's design or the figure or scene a picture depicts expresses E if and only if (1) it is an expression-look that (2) has the function, in the circumstances, of indicating E.

The theory should solve the puzzle of expressive mimesis and satisfy the connection condition. Appreciating its plausibility depends on marking the distinction between saying what an expression is and discovering its mechanisms.

Figure expression

In figure expression, a person is depicted as expressing an emotion. According to the contour theory, the expression is an expression-look that the figure is depicted as wearing and that has the function, in the circumstances, of indicating the emotion.

  Perhaps the most famous instance of the contour theory applied specifically to figure expression is Leonardo's. Leonardo thought that depicted expression is best achieved by observing and precisely copying the expressive faces and gestures of actual people (1989: 144–6). Later painters recognized that Leonardo's advice often results in figures wearing grotesque grimaces that fail to express what the figure feels: too scrupulously copying natural expressions paradoxically results in figure expressions that look wrong (e.g. the man on the far left of Fig. 13). The standard diagnosis of this failure is that natural expression-looks partly comprise movement, which cannot be captured in paint. The standard therapy prescribes several compensatory expedients (Gombrich 1982*a*).

The failure of Leonardo's advice is not a reason to reject the contour theory unless the theory implies that a depicted expression-look must resemble a natural expression-look. But, on the contrary, the theory allows that the look of a person depicted as expressing contempt may not resemble the look worn by a contemptuous-looking person seen face to face. Similarly, a man depicted as wearing a surprised look on his face need not be depicted as having the same configuration of facial features as a surprised-faced man seen *au naturel*. To look to have an expression of surprise in a picture is not always, or very often, to look just as one would look when caught face to face looking surprised.

Figure expression may avail itself of all the resources of depiction: a depicted expression may look other than it would look when seen with the naked eye. In *Fatherly Discipline*, the child's screaming face is seen simultaneously with the jagged V-shaped pen strokes with which it is drawn, and these contribute to what is expressed. What the face looks to express depends on the design in a way that has no analogue in natural expression. The lesson is that figure expression is mimetic, but mimesis does not imply illusion. When correctly stated, the contour theory solves the puzzle of mimesis for figure expression.

Without question, Leonardo's robust version of the theory promises to accomplish a task that the proposed contour theory does not. Why does the look of a depicted figure express E? By what means does it have the function of indicating E? For Leonardo, the depicted look has the function of indicating E because what is depicted resembles a natural look that has that function. Dropping Leonardo's naturalism deprives the contour theory of any account of why certain depicted looks have the function of indicating figures' emotions.

The contour theory explains only what it is for a figure to be depicted as expressing an emotion. It does not identify the mechanisms by means of which some looks have the function of indicating certain emotions. It clearly cannot provide a full understanding of pictorial expression. That, however, is no bar to accepting the theory.

Indeed, once shorn of Leonardo's naturalism, the contour theory helpfully opens up a wide view of the mechanisms of figure expression, including those that may be specifically pictorial, because there are no obvious, specific constraints on what looks can have the function of indicating what emotions. Taking a wide view increases the chance of stumbling upon non-obvious constraints. Here is a partial list of mechanisms of figure expression.

Figures may express by means of ritualized, conventional gestures. Some of these, exploited by mediaeval rhetoricians (priests giving sermons) and first codified for their training, were later used only by painters, and can be found in many Renaissance images. According to one catalogue, to signal affirmation, 'lift your arm gently...so that the back of the hand faces the beholder' (quoted in Baxandall 1988: 61)—a gesture likely to be interpreted as an insult if used nowadays as a natural expression.

Conventions of depiction, rather than conventional gestures, may also serve as mechanisms of expression. Charles Forceville (2004) has made a study of these conventions in *La Zizanie*, an Asterix comic book in which the Gauls succumb to a contagion of anger. Anger is shown by multiple superimpositions of an angry figure or by separating it from the ground plane, as if shaking; by spiral lines fanning out from the figure's head; by straight lines radiating from the mouth, as if expelling something with great force; and by smoke emanating from the angry figure's head.

Dress is rarely discussed as a vehicle of expression—consider the attire of Bruegel's dancing peasants and the variety of costumes Rembrandt wears in his self-portraits, not to mention the finely articulated expressive iconography of the eighteenth-century formal portrait. A figure can express dignity because the conventions of her dress have the function of indicating dignity.

Pictures also narrate actions, and narrative context can help determine what is expressed. The look on the Virgin's face in an

Annunciation is one of surprise, humility, and submission partly because the presence of the angel sets the narrative context. Expression and narrative often form an interpretive circle: we identify gestures as expressions of particular emotions partly by relying on the narrative context, and we make sense of the narrative context in part by seeing gestures as expressions.

A special case of expression-indicating narrative is the reactive expression of members of a chorus of onlookers. One figure's look may have the function of indicating contempt because it is directed at another figure's look of shame. The anger on the face of the father in Daumier's drawing is invisible unless it is seen as directed at the child's obstinate howling.

As these cases show, the state which a figure's look has the function of indicating may depend on what is happening nearby. Worried about the impropriety of depicting figures expressing extreme emotions, some Academic painters followed the example of Timanthes, who is said to have shown Agamemnon's grief at the sacrifice of Iphigenia by covering his face behind a veil (Crow 1999: 79–103). Only the impending sacrifice cues what emotion the gesture expresses.

Finally, what a figure looks to express may depend on properties of the picture's design. The tight, spring-like curves used to depict the figures in *Fatherly Discipline* help convey the mixture of frustration, indignant anger, and near desperation expressed by the two principal figures. The look of intense grief in Picasso's *Weeping Head* is achieved by rending and flattening the planes that make up the face, by the shape of the hand thrusting up from below, and by the intensified chiaroscuro.

Figure expression is determined by a smorgasbord of factors, some of them conventional, some of them *sui generis* (some of them may be innate). No single factor explains what gives depicted physical configurations the function of indicating one or another emotion. Figure expression is certainly not constrained to resemble natural expression. Nevertheless, it is their having emotion-indicating functions that makes them expressions.

Scene and design expression

The contour theory of figure expression is inspired by the contour theory of natural expression, and it inspires in turn a contour theory of scene and design expression. The physical configuration of a depicted scene or a pictorial design expresses an emotion, E, if and only if it has the function, in the circumstances, of indicating E. Scene and design expression are parallel, on this proposal, to figure expression.

The parallel breaks down if expression attributions imply emotion attributions, for in scene and design expression there is no depicted figure to whom any emotion can be attributed. However, the contour theory does not require that expressions be attributed to emoting figures even in the case of figure expression, so it generates no missing person problem. A depicted scene or a picture surface expresses an emotion that it does not have if it wears a look that has the function in the circumstances of indicating the emotion.

One might object that an asymmetry remains between figure expression on the one hand and scene and design expression on the other. The happy looks of depicted figures have the function of indicating the figures' happiness because their looks do or could indicate their happiness. The assumption is that no state has the function of indicating another state unless it does or could indicate that state. How can the look of a scene or design ever have the function of indicating happiness when there is never anyone whose happiness gets indicated by that look?

According to the contour theory, the mere fact that a scene or design expresses an emotion is not sufficient reason to attribute the emotion to a person—whether she be the picture's creator (actual or implied) or a non-depicted, hypothetical persona inhabiting the world of the picture. Expression attribution does not require emotion attribution. But neither does it rule it out. An emotion attribution may be warranted by the need to make sense of a narrative or an artistic purpose, for example. So we must sometimes attribute what a design or scene expresses to an undepicted person, real or hypothetical. When no attribution is made, one could be made. A look's having the function of indicating an emotion is in principle grounded in its indicating the emotion.

The strongest source of resistance to the contour theory is puzzlement about the mechanisms by means of which looks of inanimate scenes and designs have the function of indicating emotions. What is it about the brilliant sunlight illuminating the city in Turner's *Heidelberg Sunset* that makes it express joy? How do brown, black, and red come to express grave, melancholy, and terrible airs, respectively? Or why do the swirling, multi-coloured clouds in *The Scream* express psychological turmoil? How could these looks come to have the function of indicating what they do?

When it comes to natural expression, intuition reports that there is some deep, conceptual tie between expression-looks and emotions. The smile seems naturally suited to express happiness. In fact, the physical configuration that makes up a smile might have had the function of indicating disgust, surprise, or nothing at all. As long as accepting this fact runs against our intuitions about the naturalness of expressions, the question of the mechanisms of natural expression does not arise.

By contrast, the accidental nature of scene and design expression is all too obvious, and we are quickly pressed to wonder how they can be tied by resemblance to apparently less troubling natural expressions.

It was once fashionable to posit natural equivalences between properties of inanimate objects and emotions. As Gombrich puts the idea, 'every colour, sound, or shape has a natural feeling tone just as every feeling has an equivalence in the world of sight or sound' (1978:59). Others posit a similarity between looks of scenes and 'essential conditions of our physical existence' with expressive overtones such as muscular movement or gravity (Fry 1992: 85). One might think that a painting depicts a scene as joyful-looking because its clarity and bright colouration resemble the brightness of a joy-filled face.

Some of these speculations may turn out to be true. Nothing prevents me from making a picture containing a scene that is expressive because it resembles a natural expression-look. I depict the moon as sad by drawing a sad face on it, and maybe the moon has a sad look because it resembles a natural expression of sadness. (It is a separate issue whether my drawing anthropomorphizes the moon: depicting something as resembling a person does not entail depicting it as a person.)

At the same time, we need not worry if these speculations turn out to be false. After all, the expressive looks of depicted scenes or pictorial designs need not mimic natural expression-looks. No harbour, when seen face to face, looks like Munch's. Face-to-face sunsets do sometimes look like Turner's, but then they do not look as if they express joy. Depicted scenes appear to have properties they cannot appear to have when seen face to face, and pictorial expression-looks need not resemble natural expression-looks.

The contour theory says what it is for a scene or design to express. It does not catalogue the mechanisms of scene and design expression. These are separate tasks, and while both are worthy, a theory's neglecting one of them is no reason against it.

It is no reason against it if the tasks are separable. Matravers argues that they are not. Assume that facts about experience of a depicted scene must justify the judgement that the scene has a sad expression. Matravers observes that on the contour theory 'questions such as: what reason do I have to call this sad? how do I know it is sad? would admit of no more than the trivial answer that I [see] it as sad' (1998: 132). If I can say no more in justification of my judgement that a picture expresses sadness than that it looks sad, then I have reason to doubt that my judgement is justified.

It is true that the contour theory does not answer Matravers's questions. The sad expression of a depicted landscape consists in its having a look that has the function of indicating sadness, and my seeing the landscape as sad consists in my seeing it as having this look. However, the contour theory says nothing about why that look has the function of indicating sadness.

Nevertheless, the contour theory should not be faulted for failing to supply what it out-sources to another theory. There are reasons why the depicted scene has the function of indicating sadness. Good answers to the questions 'what reason do I have to call this sad? how do I know it is sad?' come from knowing the mechanisms of expression. Matravers's questions do need answers, but it does not count against the contour theory that it fails to supply them, so long as it does not imply that there are no answers.

The competition is in the same predicament. If the landscape's sadness expresses an emotion of the picture's creator, then scene expression is a special case of *sui generis* natural expression. We should be as puzzled about how a person can express his sadness by painting a greyed-out meadow as by sitting in the meadow and flipping the heads off daisies. What reason do you have to call flipping the heads off daisies a sign of sadness?

The mechanisms of emotional arousal are just as poorly understood. The tormented forms of the harbour in *The Scream* arouse feelings of existential anxiety. Why? Why not a feeling of seasickness or the desire to dance?

The hypothetical persona theory is in the worst predicament. The landscape's sad look reveals the sadness of a hypothetical persona, but why should that look reveal anyone's sadness? Ordinary mortals cannot reveal their sadness by changing the look of the planet. Nor is mother nature an empath who arranges her features to mirror the feelings of you and me. Yet attributing the emotion that a scene expresses to a hypothetical persona requires some such assumption. It is not an attribution to be taken lightly.

The robust contour theory is too ambitious, taking on a task it cannot accomplish. A better contour theory has ambitions no less modest than its competitors.

Total pessimism is unwarranted, of course. We do know something about the mechanisms of scene and design expression, although they are too unsystematic to submit to unified explanation.

We know that scene and design expression generally depend on the marked violation of norms established for the style, tradition, or genre to which a picture belongs (Gombrich 1961: 369–76; 1978).

Rembrandt paints scenes with a lot of black in them, but this does not make his paintings uniformly melancholy. Mondrian's *Broadway Boogie-Woogie* is rapturous in the context of a body of work predicated on the dictum that curves are too emotional.

Some physical configurations of scenes or designs conventionally function to indicate emotions. A familiar case is expressive colour: the spectrum from warm to cool colours is associated with a range of emotions from passionate to phlegmatic. Variations in the location of figures in a scene, placement and proportion of empty space, the relative proportions of figures and objects, the rhythm of shapes and lines, the inclination of planes, and contrast also have conventional associations with emotions.

What a scene's look has the function of expressing may also be determined by what is depicted as happening in a picture. A scene of impending, unavoidable danger can make the scene express dread. The actions or expressions of figures in a scene can also determine what the scene itself looks to express. The sea's haughty malignance in the *Raft of the Medusa* is realized in part by the sailors' battered bodies. The visual noise generated by the strong, clashing colours of the design of *Wheatfield with Crows* helps to express malevolence.

Appreciating the contour theory's plausibility means recognizing that three claims are consistent. A scene or design may express an emotion by having a certain look. It is possible that nothing has that look when viewed with the naked eye. It is possible that, when something has that look to the naked eye, it still does not express what the picture expresses. The three claims taken together explain how pictures reveal a world of expression that, without them, would remain invisible.

Seeing expressions

Figure and scene expression are achieved depictively: figures and scenes express because they are depicted as having physical configurations that are expression-looks. Not only are those configurations seen in pictures, but we see them as expressions when we see them as having the function of indicating emotions. Expressions are part of pictures' mimetic contents.

There are two ways, then, of seeing a pictorial expression. In richer cases, you see what a figure or scene expresses by seeing the expression *as an expression*. That is, you see the expression as having the function of indicating the emotion, and this requires an exercise of the emotion concept in question. In more impoverished cases, you see a physical configuration that has the function of indicating an emotion, but you do not see it as an expression—as having that function. Here no emotion concept is part of the content of expressive seeing.

The richer cases satisfy the connection condition.

Still, one might grant that although the richer cases satisfy the connection condition, they need not be mimetic. Perhaps a depicted figure or scene expresses what it does, not in so far as we *see* the figure or scene as looking haunting, but rather in so far as we see it as having a physical configuration and on that basis *judge* that it is haunting. We must infer from the look of the depicted figure or scene what emotion the look has the function of indicating.

This objection assumes that the content of a judgement inferred from what is seen in a picture cannot itself enter into the content of seeing-in. The assumption is too strong: the verdicts of inferences may become part of the mimetic content of a picture. It is an open question whether expressive judgements do in fact feed into seeing-in. Answering the question requires a theory of the contents of vision in general—something far beyond the scope of this book.

Assume, instead, that a picture may depict an object as having any property that the object may be seen to have face to face. If we see persons as having (natural) expression-looks, then we see figures or scenes in pictures as having expression-looks. If we do not see persons as having (natural) expression-looks, then we have reason to doubt that pictures express emotions at all.

Arousal and Evaluation

Nothing in the contour theory blocks the idea that some pictures
on some occasions arouse emotions in response to what they
express. Arousalism economically explains why pictures ever
arouse emotions: their arousing emotions is part of what constitutes
their expressing emotions. However, no feeling of sadness (or
anything else) is required in order to see a figure or scene as
sad-looking. So if arousal is optional, then why do we sometimes
respond emotionally to pictures, once we have taken in what they
express?

The truth is that there is no feature of a picture that arouses
its viewer's emotion in virtue of his seeing an expression-look
that is not simply a feature of a work in virtue of which he simply
sees the expression-look. The difference between a dry-eyed and
a wet-eyed response is due not to the picture but to the viewer and
his relation to the picture. Rembrandt's denial of Peter leaves the
unbeliever unmoved, and the cold-hearted psychologist examines
The Scream safe from the anxiety its expresses. Just so, the tourist
may not feel what is expressed by the figures depicted in *Fatherly
Discipline*—she may feel only gallery fatigue.

What benefits accrue to a picture's arousing an emotion, and not
merely expressing it? The question bites hard when it comes to the
arousal of emotions we normally take care to avoid, but it also arises
with positive emotions. The mystery is not only that negative
emotions can be pleasurable. We want to know how it is beneficial or
reasonable ever to be emotionally aroused by a picture, whether
positively or negatively.

Emotions are an important component of the action system: they
involve an appraisal of the environment in preparation for action
and thereby provide a motivation for acting. They also function in
the management of goals by appraising them as more or less desir-
able and by motivating taking the steps necessary to achieve them.
In addition, emotions bias thought. Happiness improves problem

solving, sadness facilitates the recall of sad events, and anxiety directs attention to dangers in the environment. What we see depends on what we feel if emotion primes attention and attention guides vision. There is no reason to think that emotional responses to pictures fail to function in these ways. This is something to keep in mind as we consider the evaluation of pictures as mimetic.

Even so, arousal's rewards do not justify a normative arousalism. On one version of this view, pictures are to be valued only for their power to arouse emotions. Thoughtful people have endorsed this proposition. Aquinas replied to iconoclastic proscriptions against the display of images in churches by remarking that images 'excite the emotions which are more effectively aroused by things seen than by things heard' (quoted in Freedberg 1989: 162). This book defends less pessimistic canons for the evaluation of pictures.

Another version of normative arousalism holds that it is always a merit in a picture that it arouses an emotion. An early formulation of this view figures among Henri Testelin's *Precepts on Expression*: 'all the parts of the Composition ought to bear the Image and Character of the Subject which we would represent; so that the Idea may pass from the Picture into the mind of those that look on it, to touch the passions which the Subject requires' (2000: 139). The trouble is that touched passions are forbidden by a picture whose full evaluation requires a measure of quiet indifference.

According to the weakest, most plausible, version of normative arousalism, expressiveness in a picture is a merit only when it actuates arousal. This is false if there is merit in simply seeing what depicted figures or scenes express.

Lurking in the wings is the puzzle of mimesis. A picture of a frustrated father can be evaluated no differently from the sight of a frustrated father if experience of expression is illusionistic. The view that the value of the picture lies in its arousing an emotional response looks appealing. Since the emotional response is aroused in the absence of an actual frustrated father, we place our hopes in catharsis, emotional clarification, and the like. However, mimetic expression is not necessarily illusionistic expression. A picture may be evaluated as a picture for presenting an expression-look quite different from an expression-look worn by anything outside pictures.

3   GOOD LOOKING

Who can see a great picture ... without taking some of the credit for it himself?

John Bayley

To evaluate a picture as a picture is in part to evaluate it as a vehicle for seeing-in. However, there are many types of evaluations of pictures as vehicles for seeing-in. It is time to consider some of them and to weigh the case for interactionism (see the Introduction). According to interactionism, there are some types of non-aesthetic evaluation, V, such that some aesthetic evaluations of pictures as vehicles for seeing-in imply or are implied by some V-evaluations of pictures as vehicles for seeing-in. Chapters 1 and 2 set the stage by describing how pictures are vehicles for seeing-in. Chapters 4 and 5 show how aesthetic evaluations of pictures interact with cognitive and moral ones. The immediate next step is to distinguish aesthetic evaluations of pictures from non-aesthetic ones. When correctly drawn, the distinction provides a test of the truth of interactionism and also completes the solution to the puzzle of mimesis.

How Good, Good How

An evaluation is a representation of something as possessing merit or demerit. What has merit is good, more or less, and nothing is good to any degree unless it is good for something. Likewise, the defective is bad, more or less, and nothing is bad to any degree unless it is bad for something. If merit and demerit are relative to purpose or activity, then so is evaluation. A knife is good when it is good at cutting, and one may praise it for cutting well. Of course, this is only one way to evaluate a knife—it might be judged more or less good at opening paint cans, for example. Since an evaluation is a representation of merit or demerit, which are relative to purpose or activity, evaluation must also take purpose or activity into account.

Although there are many ways to evaluate anything, we have a special interest in some evaluations. A knife is a cutting kind of thing, since it is designed for cutting; so when it is good at cutting, it is good as an instance of the kind of thing it is—it is good *as a knife*. A knife that is good at opening paint cans is not for that reason good as a knife. In sum, we have a special interest in evaluations of a thing as a member of the kind of thing it is.

Good as pictures

Pictures adorn public spaces, reveal the look of things, arouse emotions, afford tax-sheltering charitable donations, focus religious contemplation, mark social status, provoke political action, and serve as impromptu frisbees. Any given picture is more or less good at each of these, and may be so evaluated. Matisse's *Red Studio* is good at expressing a mood, heightening the greenness of green walls, enraging bulls, and providing philosophical examples. Some of these claims evaluate *Red Studio* as a vehicle for seeing-in; others do not. Only the former evaluate it as a picture.

As it stands, this rule is too simple to be true. On what side of the distinction fall evaluations of a picture for its focusing religious contemplation or provoking political action? An evaluation of the effectiveness of Delacroix's *Liberty on the Barricades* at stirring collective action is an evaluation of it as a picture only if it measures the picture's representational quality. Clearly, though, rousing people to action is not the same as sustaining seeing-in, and to evaluate the effectiveness of one is not the same as to evaluate the effectiveness of the other.

The solution is to upgrade the account of evaluating a picture as a picture. Let a 'picture-appropriate evaluation' be either an evaluation of a picture as sustaining seeing-in or an evaluation of it that entails an evaluation of it as sustaining seeing-in. *Liberty on the Barricades* is a masterpiece of political agitation—this is an evaluation of the picture as a picture, since it implies an evaluation of the picture's representational success. After all, it inspires action only because it depicts and thereby sustains seeing in it a scene of patriotic courage and defiance. An evaluation is an evaluation of a picture as a picture if and only if it is a picture-appropriate evaluation of the picture.

For the sake of convenience, focus only on evaluations of pictures as vehicles of seeing-in. The restriction is harmless as long as we keep in mind that some evaluations of pictures as pictures merely imply evaluations of them as vehicles for seeing-in.

The proposition that to evaluate a picture as a picture is to evaluate it as a vehicle for seeing-in may be read as an instance of one of several conceptions of evaluation-as (Vermazen 1988). The strongest is

exclusion: to evaluate a member of a kind K as a K is at least in part to evaluate it with respect to a property *only* possessed by Ks.

On this conception of evaluation-as, to evaluate a picture as a picture is at least in part to evaluate it as regards a feature unique to pictures. The question to address is whether pictures alone can serve as vehicles for seeing-in. Somewhat weaker is

excellence: to evaluate a K as a K is at least in part to evaluate it with respect to a property *especially effectively realized* in Ks.

Some properties possessed by objects of many kinds are effectively realized by members of one kind. If seeing-in is not unique to pictures, but rather finds especially effective expression in them, then to evaluate a picture as a picture is to evaluate it as a vehicle for seeing-in.

Exclusion and excellence being too strong, we need only endorse

essentialism: to evaluate a K as a K is at least in part to evaluate it with respect to a property necessarily possessed by Ks.

Essentialism implies that if to evaluate a picture as a picture is to evaluate it (in part) as a vehicle for seeing-in, then all pictures are vehicles for seeing-in. We have assumed that all pictures are indeed vehicles for seeing-in (see the Introduction).

The mimesis thesis and pictorial evaluation thesis govern our conception of pictorial evaluation. To evaluate a picture as a picture is to evaluate it as a mimetic representation—one that sustains seeing-in. This principle does not say that pictures are good as pictures to the degree that they are worth seeing-in *tout court.* There are circumstances in which no picture is worth seeing-in—*Guernica* is not worth looking at in hell, for example (Ziff 1958: 225). Rather, the principle is that, all things being equal, a picture is good as a picture in so far as it is worth having the scene-presenting experience it elicits. In the negative case, a picture is bad as a picture, all things being equal, in so far as it is not worth having the scene-presenting experience it elicits.

The principle is not essentially aesthetic, however. A picture may have merit as a picture because it enables members of her fan club to know, for example, what Oprah Winfrey looks like—but that is not an aesthetic evaluation of the picture. To say what it is to evaluate a picture *as a picture* is not yet to say what it is to evaluate it *aesthetically.*

Aesthetic Evaluation

An aesthetic evaluation is a type of representation. It may have a distinctive type of object, a distinctive content, a distinctive source, or a distinctive role.

Aesthetic evaluation as art evaluation

That an evaluation of a picture is an evaluation of it as a picture does not make the evaluation an aesthetic one. Perhaps, though, aesthetic evaluation is evaluation of an object as another, special kind of object—a work of art. On this view, an aesthetic evaluation of a picture is one that measures its value not merely as a picture but more specifically as a pictorial artwork (Strawson 1974). The proposal is deflationary, since it reduces aesthetic evaluation to the evaluation of works of the art kind. In this way it promises to capitalize on the remarkable recent advances made in theorizing about art.

Notice that deflationism with respect to moral judgements is not so tempting. It is hard to see how moral evaluations could be cast as evaluations of an independently characterized proper subset of actions, characters, or institutions, since any action, character, or institution is potentially subject to moral evaluation. However, this is not an objection to aesthetic deflationism. Maybe it is a feature of aesthetic evaluation that it is deflatable in a way that has no parallel in the case of moral evaluation.

The first good reason to resist deflationism is that it parochializes the aesthetic, implying that all aesthetic evaluation is evaluation of things as artworks. Deflationism overlooks the gap between art, as we normally think of it, and the class of things which we customarily evaluate aesthetically. Some things in this class are not artefacts at all—unadorned human bodies and unbuilt landscapes, for example. The point retains its force when applied to pictures: some pictures are properly evaluated aesthetically although they seem not to be works of art. Examples include some technical drawings, doodles, and holiday snapshots.

One reply simply denies the gap; another attempts to explain it. Denying the gap, one may insist that our pre-theoretic conceptions of art or aesthetic evaluation are mistaken: either unbuilt landscapes or snapshots are art, or they cannot be said to have aesthetic value. So much the worse for intuitions. Explaining the gap, one might suggest that things that are not art can be evaluated as art. Just as a knife can be judged good at paint-can opening although it is not a paint-can opener, so an unbuilt landscape can be evaluated as art though it is not art. Evaluation *as* art does not imply evaluation *of* art.

The second reply, as much as the first, denies intuitions about a gap between art and the aesthetic. It is counterintuitive that we think of aesthetic evaluations of an unbuilt landscape or holiday snapshot as art evaluations. We do not think that to value a sunset we must think of it as an artefact. The proposal does violence to ordinary thinking about sunsets. Perhaps, as an alternative, an evaluation of something as art need not be an evaluation of it as an artefact made by a person working in the tradition of an art-form in a given social setting. But in that case we lose any theoretic benefits that might have been brought to an account of aesthetic evaluation from an account of art evaluation.

We may be better off having revised our intuitions. That it spawns revisionism does not refute deflationism, but it does show that we have no reason to accept it unless it provides a better account of aesthetic evaluation than its competitors. A final verdict must wait upon an assessment of the competition.

A second worry about deflationism is that it imperializes the aesthetic by implying that any evaluation of an artwork as art is aesthetic evaluation.

Some evaluations of pictures as works of pictorial art seem not to be aesthetic—they are pragmatic, cognitive, or moral. *Liberty on the Barricades* is good at mobilizing the people (and this is partly why it is prized as art); *Woman with Field Glasses* is good at provoking thought about the male gaze (and this is partly why it is prized as art); and *Guernica* powerfully condemns a terrible evil (and this is partly why it is prized as art). It appears that the same merits may accrue to a massacre, a culture studies textbook, and an anti-war tract, and a finding of merit in each case is clearly not an aesthetic evaluation.

According to deflationism, this is an illusion. The evaluations of *Woman* and *Ways of Seeing* may look alike, but the former is aesthetic and the latter is not, because *Woman* is art and *Ways of Seeing* is a textbook. An evaluation is aesthetic when it is an evaluation of an artwork as art, even if very similar evaluations of non-art objects are not aesthetic. We are stripped of our ability to classify evaluations in a natural way—to see that *Liberty* and a massacre can be evaluated in the same way and hence to see some evaluations of artworks as non-aesthetic. What appears to be an embrace of a pluralist recognition that pictures can be evaluated in many ways is in fact a bloated monism.

This result is fatal if the purpose of the distinction between aesthetic and non-aesthetic evaluations is to assess interactionism. Unless it is possible to distinguish different types of evaluations of artworks as art, interactionism is trivially true. What looks like a cognitive evaluation of a work—for example, '*Guernica* tells the truth about war'—is an aesthetic evaluation because it is an evaluation of the painting as art.

Moreover, the second worry buttresses the first. If deflationism is uninformative, then it enjoys no greater explanatory power than its competitors, and in that case its revisionism is untenable.

Deflationism proposes that aesthetic evaluation has a distinctive type of object. Alternatives give it a distinctive content, source, or role.

Evaluation and value

One account of what makes an evaluation aesthetic has two virtues rarely combined, for it is both obvious and true. An evaluation is a representation of something as possessing merit or demerit, so an evaluation is aesthetic if and only if it represents an object as possessing aesthetic merit or demerit (Urmson 1957). An aesthetic evaluation is an attribution of aesthetic value. Aesthetic evaluations are representations distinguished by their contents.

Unfortunately, what is true and obvious is not always enough. We seek an account of aesthetic evaluation that distinguishes it from non-aesthetic evaluation so as eventually to be able to assess the viability of interactionism. Interactionism is viable only if, for some pictures, an explanation of their aesthetic merit or demerit entails their having non-aesthetic merit or demerit, such as cognitive or moral merit. Knowing whether this condition is met requires an account of the features that, in any given circumstances, confer aesthetic merit or demerit. A defence of interactionism could then proceed by showing that, in some cases, those features are ones that also confer a non-aesthetic merit or demerit. The trouble is that nothing like such an account of aesthetic value exists.

Two elements of the work of Frank Sibley on aesthetic evaluations are so widely endorsed that they may be safely followed (other views of Sibley are contested). First, there are two kinds of aesthetic evaluations, each embedding a different kind of aesthetic concept. Second, the application of aesthetic concepts is governed only by negative conditions.

Substantive aesthetic evaluations embed substantive aesthetic concepts such as those named in Sibley's famous list: 'unified, balanced, integrated, lifeless, serene, sombre, dynamic, powerful, vivid, delicate, moving, trite, sentimental, tragic' (2001*a*: 1).

Complicating matters, some of these terms are ambiguous, sometimes naming aesthetic properties, otherwise naming non-aesthetic properties. 'Graceful, delicate, dainty, handsome, comely, elegant, garish' are typically aesthetic, whereas 'red, noisy, brackish, clammy, square, docile, curved, evanescent, intelligent, faithful, derelict, tardy, freakish' are sometimes but seldom aesthetic (Sibley 2001*a*: 2). Moreover, Sibley holds that some substantive aesthetic concepts are descriptive rather than evaluative.

To simplify, overlook the ambiguity of aesthetic terms and treat substantive aesthetic concepts as evaluative—as figuring in evaluations. The simplification is harmless as long as it is proposed in service of an account of aesthetic evaluation rather than non-evaluative aesthetic experience or aesthetic description.

Given the simplification, it is helpful to think of substantive aesthetic concepts as thick (Williams 1985: 141–3; Gibbard 1992). Thick concepts have descriptive components in the sense that they track a work's representational, expressive, or formal features. However, to apply the concepts is not only to track these features; it is also to identify the features as merits or flaws of the work. Thus to see the *Mona Lisa* as evocative or a Warhol silkscreen as hyperbolic is in each case to see the work as having features whereby it has merit, as to see a Lichtenstein riff on a comic book as mysterious or *Desmoiselles d'Avignon* as chaotic is in each case to see the work as having features whereby it is defective. 'Evocative', 'hyperbolic', 'mysterious', and 'chaotic' are thick concepts deployed in substantive aesthetic evaluations.

Sibley assumes that some concepts are substantive aesthetic concepts and others are not, and that we know which are which—he never attempts a definition of substantive aesthetic concepts. True, one might go ahead and define aesthetic evaluations as ones embedding aesthetic concepts—hence attributing aesthetic value—without having first defined aesthetic concepts. However, no definition of this sort suffices to test interactionism. The view's opponents, when confronted with a case in which a substantive aesthetic evaluation allegedly implies or is implied by a non-aesthetic evaluation, are free to deny that the former evaluation is genuinely aesthetic—to deny that it embeds a genuine substantive aesthetic concept. A definition of aesthetic concepts is needed to counter this reply.

One solution defines substantive aesthetic evaluations as those that neither imply nor are implied by non-aesthetic evaluations (Beardsley 1981). Those attracted by this solution usually think of aesthetic concepts as strictly formal ones, such as 'unity' and 'coherence'.

Not only is this solution objectionable in itself but, more importantly, it begs the question against interactionism. Driven to despair by the teeming variety of concepts on Sibley's list, one might be tempted to winnow from the list anything that might have logical concourse with non-aesthetic concepts. The abridged list that issues from this procedure will comprise only aesthetic concepts, and perhaps that is progress, but it is extensionally adequate only if interactionism is false.

According to Sibleyan orthodoxy, aesthetic evaluations come in two kinds. One is substantive; a second comprises verdicts—assessments of the overall aesthetic merit or demerit of a work. Verdicts embed thin or purely evaluative, non-descriptive aesthetic concepts: to apply them is only to evaluate. Since to call a work 'beautiful', 'nice', or 'worthless' is to evaluate it without saying anything about the features in virtue of which it is beautiful, nice, or worthless, evaluations containing these terms embed thin concepts.

Another solution defines substantive aesthetic evaluations as those that imply, explain, or justify aesthetic verdicts. For this solution to work, some account is needed of thin aesthetic concepts. If there is no more to say about aesthetic verdicts than that they represent aesthetic merit and demerit, then it is an open question whether any given evaluation is a substantive aesthetic evaluation. Notoriously, the route leading to an account of thin aesthetic concepts is littered with corpses.

Aesthetic merit has long been identified with beauty, and aesthetic demerit with ugliness. While Wittgenstein went too far in calling the view that aesthetics is the science of the beautiful 'almost too ridiculous for words' (1967: 11), the traditional thought hardly helps. On the one hand, anyone may use 'beauty' as a synonym for 'aesthetic merit' and 'ugliness' as a synonym for 'aesthetic demerit', but substitution is not explanation. On the other hand, when 'beauty' and 'ugliness' function as substantive concepts and have partly descriptive application conditions, they are not coextensive with 'aesthetic merit' and 'aesthetic demerit'. The ugliness of some paintings by Francis Bacon contributes to their overall aesthetic merit, and many a picture is ruined, aesthetically, by its beauty.

Some have thought that aesthetic value is tied to pleasure, so that a work has aesthetic merit in so far as it delivers a shot of pleasure. Again, this will not do. A picture may have aesthetic merit in virtue of (not despite) the fact that it is unpleasantly 'disturbing, dizzying, despairing, disorienting' (Levinson 1996*b*: 12). Consider *Woman with Field Glasses* (Fig. 2) and *Fatherly Discipline* (Fig. 8) as examples. Pictures may please when they have aesthetic merit, but their pleasing is not in general what makes them aesthetically meritorious.

A history of failure is no reason to concede defeat. A workable theory of aesthetic value may lie around the corner, but nobody knows now what that theory is, and nothing compels us to define aesthetic evaluation in terms of aesthetic value if aesthetic value (or aesthetic value concepts) is not well understood. Indeed, it is possible that an understanding of aesthetic evaluation will facilitate the task of understanding aesthetic value.

Evaluation and experience

The pleasure theory of aesthetic value is a special case of a more plausible theory, aesthetic empiricism, which has many advocates—but also a few opponents (Beardsley 1979; Iseminger 1981; Budd 1995; Levinson 1996*b*; cf. Stecker 1997: 251–8; versus Sharpe 2000; David Davies 2004: 253–62; Shelley 2004). The jury is still out on aesthetic empiricism, but giving some thought to its appeal suggests a way forward.

According to aesthetic empiricism, the aesthetic value of a work is tied to the value of experiences that the work elicits. More specifically, a picture or other work has aesthetic (de)merit because and to the degree that it causes or is able to cause experiences with intrinsic (i.e. non-instrumental) value. The source of aesthetic value is an intrinsically valuable experience; a picture is made valuable, aesthetically, by the value of the experiences it is able to evoke. Only aesthetic value has this source. This is its distinguishing mark.

The pleasure theory of aesthetic value adds to aesthetic empiricism the claim that the experiences of a picture that are the source of its aesthetic merit are intrinsically valuable in so far as they are pleasurable (and the experiences of a work that are the source of its aesthetic demerit lack intrinsic value in so far as they are not pleasant). The trouble with the pleasure theory is that degree of pleasure does not covary with aesthetic merit.

The remedy is to acknowledge the many kinds of intrinsic merit that accrue to experiences of aesthetically good pictures. Jerrold Levinson, in rejecting the pleasure theory, endorses a pluralistic aesthetic empiricism, writing that experience of a work may be intrinsically worthwhile,

because one's cognitive faculties are notably exercised or enlarged; because one's eyes or ears are opened to certain spatial and temporal possibilities; because one is enabled to explore unusual realms of emotion; because one's consciousness is integrated to a degree out of the ordinary; because one is afforded a distinctive feeling of freedom or transcendence; because certain moral truths are made manifest to one in concrete dress; or because one is provided insight, in one way or another, into human nature. (1996b: 19)

Setting aside quibbles about the exact items on this list, some works are valuable because they may cause many of the kinds of experiences that Levinson enumerates.

The fact that works are valuable for causing or having the capacity to cause valuable experiences is not by itself proof of aesthetic empiricism, however. While endorsing Levinson's list, one might deny that the aesthetic value of works consists in their causing the valuable experiences. One might reverse the order of priority, saying that the experiences listed are valuable only because they find the value of the works experienced. Getting right the order of priority is no easy matter. It is likely to require an antecedent understanding of the role of attributions of aesthetic value and the relationship between attributions of aesthetic value and attributions of other kinds of value. This is exactly what we are trying to learn.

An alternative to settling the status of aesthetic empiricism attempts to capture its appeal without making a commitment to it.

As is often repeated, Baumgarten originally used 'aesthetics' in 1735 to name 'the science of how things are to be cognized by means of the senses' (quoted in Guyer 1998: 227). Therefore suppose that the aesthetic is tied to experience, especially sensuous or perceptual experience. Nobody denies this very weak claim. The challenge is to characterize the tie in a way that is informative and yet entails no commitment to anything as contentious as aesthetic empiricism.

Aesthetic empiricism characterizes the tie externalistically. Intrinsically valuable experience is the source of, and so external to, the aesthetic value of a work. Aesthetic evaluation, if it is a representation of aesthetic value, is at two removes from intrinsically valuable experience. An aesthetic evaluation attributes a merit to a work, and it is justified if the work's merit is rooted in an intrinsically valuable experience the work causes.

Those who reject aesthetic empiricism frequently share its externalist characterization of experiences of works. Works, they grant, do engender experiences that are more or less valuable, but the aesthetic value of the works is not a matter of the value of the experiences. At best, the value of the experience allows us to access or measure the value of the work.

Another view, hinted at by Peter Kivy, is weaker than aesthetic empiricism but is also externalist (1989: 114–16). Kivy stipulates a sense in which aesthetic evaluations are those evaluations to which only aesthetic properties are relevant, where aesthetic properties are sensual or perceptible structural properties (see also Levinson 1990: 183). The view is externalist, since aesthetic properties are experiential and are tied to aesthetic evaluation by a relevance relation.

According to internalism, experience is part of aesthetic evaluation. How it is part of aesthetic evaluation will take some explaining. Meanwhile, note that this view is not committed to aesthetic empiricism: the experience in question need not be valuable, and if it is valuable, its value need not explain the value of the work experienced.

Experiential Internalism

Aesthetic evaluations cannot be distinguished from non-aesthetic evaluations by their objects. They can be defined as evaluations embedding concepts that attribute aesthetic value, but this definition is not helpful in testing interactionism. A look at the role of aesthetic evaluation in criticism sheds light on evaluative experience.

Appreciation and experience

Aesthetic evaluations have their home in critical discourse. One common understanding of the purpose of criticism is so narrow, however, that it encourages an atrophied conception of the role of aesthetic evaluation. A more expansive understanding of criticism as aiming at appreciation grounds a conception of the role of aesthetic evaluation that highlights what is distinctive to it.

Criticism is commonly thought to aim at and, when successful, culminate in the issuing of verdicts. Journalistic art criticism, especially movie, theatre, and book reviews, typically terminates in an overall evaluation of a work's merit, intended to guide consumer choice. The star system in movie reviews is a striking instance of verdict-oriented criticism.

At the same time, however, a great deal of thoughtful and sophisticated criticism rarely issues verdicts and centres instead on substantive aesthetic evaluations. Indeed, much criticism of pictures is not verdict-oriented. No doubt the reason is that the choice to look at any given picture has a relatively low cost—it is possible to look at a great many pictures in a brief span of time, which is not the case with watching a movie or a play, or reading a book.

One might object that in all picture criticism verdicts are implicit when not explicit. When implicit, they can be deduced from explicit judgements that are not verdicts. This is too optimistic. Verdict-free criticism often highlights merits and flaws in a work that do not add up to a clear verdict; and there may be no method for weighing merits and defects so as to measure the overall value of a work (Vermazen 1975).

Even verdict-oriented criticism, or much of it, does not function solely to sustain verdicts. The point of issuing a verdict is sometimes to invite more fine-grained, substantive observations. In these cases, verdicts invite substantive aesthetic evaluations and do not function to terminate discourse.

In sum, substantive aesthetic evaluations dominate criticism that is not verdict-oriented and also verdict-oriented criticism in which verdicts do not function to terminate discourse. Yet in each case, criticism must serve a useful purpose. This is puzzling as long as we think of criticism, and hence aesthetic evaluation, as demonstrative.

On the demonstrative model of criticism, aesthetic evaluations are aesthetic judgements (that is, beliefs) that are apt to be asserted. For this reason they are suited to figure in pieces of reasoning in which purely descriptive judgements or substantive aesthetic judgements are reasons for judging that a work has some degree of overall aesthetic value. The judgement that the painting is beautiful is warranted by the judgement that it is gracefully intelligent. In some cases a verdict is implied by a substantive aesthetic evaluation, but demonstration does not require implication. Sometimes purely descriptive judgements or substantive aesthetic judgements warrant a verdict by explaining the verdict. That a work is gracefully intelligent may warrant my judging it beautiful because it explains how the work is beautiful. In each case, aesthetic judgements provide reasons to judge.

The demonstrative model predicts that critical discourse aims to terminate in verdicts, and we are puzzled when criticism appears inconsistent with this aim.

Tradition acknowledges an alternative to the demonstrative model. Arnold Isenberg distinguished critical communication from ordinary communication, which comprises assertions whose purpose is to give the speaker's audience reasons to believe what is asserted. For Isenberg, 'communication is a process by which a mental content is transmitted by symbols from one person to another', whereas 'it is a function of criticism to bring about communication at the level of the senses, that is, to induce a sameness of vision, of experienced content' (1949: 336). The critic is therefore 'one who affords new perceptions and with them new values' (Isenberg 1949: 341). Stuart Hampshire observed a decade later that 'one engages in aesthetic discussion for the sake of what one might see on the way, and not for the sake of arriving at a conclusion, a final verdict for and against; if one has been brought to see what there is to be seen in the object, the purpose of discussion is achieved' (1959: 165). The point is reiterated in a strain of Sibley, who remarks that 'an activity the successful outcome of which is seeing … cannot … be called reasoning' (2001*b*:40). Of course, Sibley is employing a narrow conception of reasoning. Hume thought that 'in many orders of beauty, particularly those of the finer arts, it is requisite to employ much reasoning in order to find the proper sentiment; and a false relish may frequently be corrected by argument and reflection' (1777: 137). Only conceived broadly—as not merely demonstrative—do reasoning, argument, and reflection yield proper sentiment and relish.

This model of criticism explains why some criticism is either not verdict-oriented or else not structured so as to terminate in verdicts. Verdicts do not offer precise guidance towards rich and accurate appreciative experiences. The point is not that all criticism is appreciative (it is not) or that verdicts are unimportant in criticism (they are important). Rather, acknowledging that some criticism is appreciative inspires an alternative model of aesthetic evaluation.

First, aesthetic evaluations need not be judgements, though they may occasionally take the form of judgements. Second, aesthetic evaluations need not be potential elements of reasoning structures in which some evaluations imply or explain or warrant others.

Critical discourse sometimes draws evaluative attention to features of works. It guides the application of aesthetic concepts and prompts experiences of objects as valuable in certain respects. Thus aesthetic evaluations of pictures may be visual experiences of pictures as valuable in this respect or that. On this view, critical commentary on pictures is not geared only to pronouncing verdicts; it also works to make evaluative experiences available to those who look at pictures.

The internalist conjecture

The appreciation model of criticism suggests that aesthetic evaluation sometimes amounts to seeing value. It sometimes takes the form of experiences of pictures as valuable—it is not merely a result of these experiences. In a nutshell, experience is internal to evaluation. The following conjecture cracks the nut.

Letting 'P' stand for any picture and 'F' for any property (such as 'square', 'insipid', or 'beautiful'), the internalist conjecture holds that

an evaluation, R, of P as F is an aesthetic evaluation if and only if, were R accurate, (1) being F would be a (de)merit in P, all else being equal; (2) a suitable observer's experience, E, of P as F is partly constitutive of (1); and (3) R is an experience with the same content as E or R is a representation warranted by E.

I see *Moonlit Kittens* as sentimental. My experience is an aesthetic evaluation just in case each of three conditions is satisfied. First, if my experience is accurate, then the sentimentality of *Moonlit Kittens* is one of its faults. Second, a suitable observer's seeing *Moonlit Kittens* as sentimental is partly constitutive of the fact that the sentimentality of *Moonlit Kittens* is one of its faults. Third, my experience has the same content as the experience of the suitable observer. Looking at the picture, I blurt out, '*Moonlit Kittens* ... how sentimental.' This is also an aesthetic evaluation: it is not an experience with the same content as a suitable observer's, but it is warranted by that experience.

The first point to note is that, as formulated here, the internalist conjecture applies only to pictures. It may also apply to works in other media and to natural objects, but it would be a mistake to take for granted that it can be generalized. The sticking point, as we shall see below, is the interpretation of 'experience' in clause (2).

The conjecture concerns types of evaluation and distinguishes one type from others. The assertion 'That picture is sentimental' is an evaluation if it is a finding of merit or demerit—if 'sentimental' is a thick concept. However, the assertion may be read as a representation which does not attribute merit or demerit. The conjecture does nothing to distinguish purely descriptive aesthetic representations from other types of representation.

Clause (1) says that an aesthetic evaluation of a picture represents it as having a property and that, as a matter of fact, it is a merit or demerit in the picture that it has the property. If my blurting out

'That picture is sentimental' is an aesthetic evaluation, then my assertion represents the picture as sentimental, and it is a fact that its being sentimental is a (de)merit in it. However, this holds only for evaluations that are accurate. Some aesthetic evaluations are inaccurate. The judgement '*Woman Holding a Balance* is chaotic' is not accurate, though it appears to be an aesthetic evaluation. The first clause accommodates this: in possible worlds where the evaluation is accurate, the picture's being chaotic is a demerit, all else being equal.

Note also that the (de)merit is not specifically aesthetic. The purpose of the conjecture is to distinguish aesthetic from non-aesthetic evaluations so as to evaluate interactionism, and this purpose would be undermined were aesthetic evaluation defined as the representation of aesthetic (de)merit.

It is in clause (2) that internalism makes its appearance. It states that part of what it is for sentimentality to be a flaw in *Moonlit Kittens* is that someone has an experience of *Kittens* as sentimental. That experience is perceptual or quasi-perceptual (Lopes 2003*a*). If the conjecture applies to works in other media or to natural objects, then the experience need not be visual. When it comes to pictures, the experience is nevertheless *visual*.

This language in clause (2) about partial constitution requires caution on two fronts. First, the claim is not that the experience of *Kittens* as sentimental is part of what it is for the picture to be senti-mental. Nor is it that an experience of the sentimentality as a flaw is part of what makes the picture's sentimentality a flaw. As we shall see, when read in either of these ways, the conjecture fails to distin-guish aesthetic evaluation from other types of evaluation. The claim advanced in clause (2) is that the experience of *Kittens* as sentimental is part of what it is for the picture's sentimentality to be a flaw in it. Here are three facts: (i) *Kittens* is sentimental, (ii) *Kittens* is experienced as sentimental, and (iii) being sentimental is a flaw in *Kittens*. The conjecture says that (ii) partly constitutes (iii).

Second, not just anybody's experience will do; the experience must be one enjoyed by a suitable observer. There is no need for present purposes to lay down in any detail who counts as a suitable observer and why. Nevertheless, some minimal constraints are needed if appeal to a suitable observer is to inject a normative element into the conjecture. We ought to respond as the suitable observer does, because she embodies our standards for good looking.

One minimum constraint is that the suitable observer's experiences arise from and reflect an accurate understanding of the picture. She must be sensitive to the effects of the picture and possess whatever discrimination skills and background knowledge sensitivity requires, including background knowledge of other paintings and the relevant pictorial idiom (Walton 1970). Mondrian's *Broadway Boogie-Woogie* is seen to be lively only in the context of his other, more austere grids. Considerable experience is needed to discriminate the subtle differences between Chardin's still lifes.

Moreover, the suitable observer must resemble you and me in respect of certain basic cognitive abilities. After all, the conjecture implies that '*Kittens* is sentimental' is not an aesthetic evaluation unless 'being sentimental' is a property that can be seen in *Kittens*. Yet it is contingent that this property is one that can be represented in human visual experience (my dog, Nico, cannot see anything as sentimental). Thus the suitable observer must be capable of having visual experiences with the kinds of contents that our visual experiences can have. (Nico is not a good candidate.)

The conjecture's third clause accommodates the idea that aesthetic evaluations may take the form of experiences. In conjunction with the second clause, it suggests that aesthetic evaluations are experiences in central cases. Indeed, they are type-identical to the experiences of the suitable observer mentioned in clause (2). When you are a suitable observer whose experience of *Kittens* as sentimental is an aesthetic evaluation, clause (3) is satisfied trivially—E just is R.

Clause (3) also allows that aesthetic evaluations may be judgements (that is, beliefs), thoughts, assertions, or unasserted statements. Aesthetic evaluations, when they take one of these forms, derive from the central cases by a relation of warrant.

Aesthetic, non-aesthetic

A full argument for the internalist conjecture would show that it best explains interesting epistemic and metaphysical features of aesthetic value, aesthetic concepts, and aesthetic evaluation; but nobody knows what the features are that stand in need of explanation. Even so, enough can be said in favour of the conjecture to use it to test interactionism. It is modest, accommodating many views on the aesthetic, affording little reason to reject it on sight. It is also informative, discriminating all and only cases of aesthetic evaluation.

Testing interactionism requires a principled way of distinguishing aesthetic from non-aesthetic evaluations. The conjecture fills this need if it is extensionally adequate. Indeed, something less than full extensional adequacy will suffice. Interactionists are not interested in demonstrating that there are logical connections between aesthetic evaluations and just *any* non-aesthetic evaluations. What matters are relationships between aesthetic evaluations on the one hand and cognitive and moral evaluations on the other. So the conjecture must above all distinguish aesthetic evaluations from cognitive and moral ones.

Needless to say, there is little agreement on the precise location of the boundaries of aesthetic evaluation. The best we can hope to show is that the conjecture correctly distinguishes clear cases of aesthetic evaluation from clear cases of non-aesthetic evaluation. Unless some evaluations of pictures are non-aesthetic, interactionism is trivially true. Furthermore, the conjecture should not rule out from the start any overlap between aesthetic and non-aesthetic evaluations of pictures—otherwise interactionism is false by definition. It is enough if the conjecture distinguishes those aesthetic evaluations from those non-aesthetic evaluations that are not in dispute between interactionists and autonomists.

Begin by assuming that aesthetic evaluations do satisfy the internalist conjecture. Do some non-aesthetic evaluations fail to satisfy it? In answering this question, it is wise to consider evaluations of items other than pictures where they provide the paradigm instances of non-aesthetic evaluation. Let 'P' in the conjecture stand for any object.

An easy first case is pragmatic evaluation. Sharpness is a virtue in a knife when it is evaluated as a knife, but the knife's being experienced (seen or felt) to be sharp is not part of what it is for the sharpness to be a virtue in the knife. The merit of sharpness in a knife is quite independent of anybody's experience of its sharpness. Therefore the judgement that the knife is sharp is not an aesthetic evaluation.

More interesting are cases of cognitive evaluation. Suppose that being warranted is a merit of your belief, and you judge that your belief is warranted. That is a cognitive evaluation. However, being warranted is a merit of your belief no matter whether you or anyone else *experiences* your belief as warranted—keep in mind that 'experience' is perceptual or quasi-perceptual. So-called internalists about warrant claim that a belief is not warranted unless someone knows or believes that it is warranted, and they might add that unless this condition obtains, the warrant is not a merit either. Be that as it may, the warrant of your belief is no less a merit of it if nobody sees (or visualizes) it as warranted. So the judgement that your belief is warranted is not an aesthetic evaluation.

The internalist conjecture also distinguishes aesthetic from moral evaluations. Take an evaluation of an action as beneficent. Being beneficent is a merit in the action. Yet it is no part of the meritoriousness of an action's beneficence that the action is seen or otherwise experienced as beneficent. The point is not that an action cannot be seen to be beneficent. Maybe when you see a man help another in need your visual experience represents him as beneficent. Nevertheless, the meritoriousness of the action's beneficence does not depend on anyone's having an experience like this. Analogous points can be made about the moral evaluation of characters and institutions.

Many believe that moral properties are response-dependent. They say that the man's action is not beneficent unless it is represented in some way by some person as beneficent, or it is not meritorious unless it is represented in some way by some person as meritorious. They may also say that the action's beneficence is not a merit in it unless the action is represented in some way by some person as beneficent. For all that, nobody holds that the form which the representation must take is experiential. What distinguishes aesthetic from non-aesthetic evaluation is that only the former is necessarily tied to experience.

Intuitions are more likely to be upset by the application of the conjecture to hedonic evaluations—evaluations of things as pleasurable or painful, where pleasure and pain are experienced. Caetan takes a fall and reports 'Ow!' The report seemingly satisfies the criteria for being an aesthetic evaluation. It is a bad thing that the fall hurt. Part of what it is for the fall's painfulness to be bad is that Caetan experiences the fall as painful. If he did not experience it as painful, then it would not be the case that its painfulness were bad. This assumes that Caetan is a suitable observer. Surely he is. Who better? Consider the third-person analogue. Seeing Caetan fall, I say, 'That hurt'. All the same, part of what it is for the fall's painfulness to be bad is that *Caetan* experiences it as painful. My assertion is warranted by his experience. So it seems that hedonic evaluations are aesthetic.

The price of biting that bullet is not obviously too high to bear. There does seem to be some link between the aesthetic and the hedonic. For Kant (1987), aesthetic evaluation is a genus divided into two species—judgements of taste attributing beauty and judgements of the agreeable attributing pleasurableness and painfulness. We might welcome the internalist conjecture as one way to capture Kant's insight that the two types of evaluation are of a kind.

A welcoming attitude need not obscure the differences between evaluations such as 'The painting is insipid' and 'The massage is nice'. Acknowledging the differences may also satisfy those unable to resist the intuition that hedonic evaluations are not aesthetic.

For one thing, there is a sense in which Caetan's experience of his fall as painful is wholly, not merely partly, constitutive of the badness of the fall's hurting. In this sense, the badness of the fall's hurting does not depend on anything but Caetan's experience of it as hurting. One might make it a condition upon hedonic evaluation that the (de)merit of a pleasurable or painful event is wholly constituted by an experience of it as pleasurable or painful. The internalist conjecture may be amended to require that a suitable observer's experience of P as F be partly *and not wholly* constitutive of F being a (de)merit in P. Thus hedonic evaluations are not aesthetic if an event's hedonic value is wholly constituted by an experience of it as pleasurable or painful.

In addition, we have seen that in the case of hedonic evaluations the suitable observer is always the person who experiences the pleasure or pain. It is merely their experiencing the pleasure or pain that qualifies them for that role. By contrast, that '*Kittens* is sentimental' is an aesthetic evaluation does not require that any particular person occupy the role of suitable observer. There is a special constraint on who may count as a suitable observer in the case of Caetan that does not constrain the case of *Kittens*.

It may or may not be better to class hedonic evaluations with aesthetic ones. Testing interactionism does not require that we decide. After all, nobody seriously denies that some aesthetic evaluations of pictures do imply evaluations of their capacity to please or displease. Put another way, the fact that evaluating interactionism does not compel us to settle the matter means that it is hard to see what in the present context could decide it.

We have assumed that the conjecture is satisfied by all aesthetic evaluations—or all central cases of them. Examples include seeing *Woman Holding a Balance* as delicate and judging that *Fatherly Discipline* is unsettling. It is time to discharge the assumption.

One worry is that while some aesthetic evaluations do satisfy the internalist conjecture, others do not. Here is a candidate: '*Woman with Field Glasses* is original' (see Vermazen 1991; Sibley 2001*c*). Presumably many people will classify this as an aesthetic evaluation (albeit there are some non-evaluative uses of 'original'). However, nothing can be seen as original. Originality is a historical property that does not supervene on a picture's look and so is invisible. Ergo aesthetic evaluations need not attribute perceptible properties.

The immediate reply is to deny that attributions of originality and other historical properties to works are aesthetic evaluations. When they are evaluative, they evaluate works as artefacts—they are art evaluations. Likewise, attributions of such properties as 'derivativeness, skillfulness, revolutionariness, typicality, influentiality, syntheticness, distinctiveness of vision' (Levinson 1990: 183). These are art evaluations rather than aesthetic evaluations. If the intuitive boundaries of aesthetic evaluation are fuzzy at all points, they are downright messy where they abut the intuitive boundaries of art evaluation. We have little reason in this case to treat our intuitions as germane. Moreover, our intuitions are easily honoured if they are interpreted as intuitions about art evaluation.

In favour of this reply is the fact that some relational properties can be attributed to pictures in aesthetic evaluations. Suppose I judge that *Moonlit Kittens* is more sentimental than *Sunset Lovers*. 'Being more sentimental than *Sunset Lovers*' is not intrinsic to *Kittens*, and does not supervene on the look of *Kittens*. But it does supervene on the looks of *Kittens* and *Sunset* together, and this explains why it properly figures in an aesthetic evaluation. The internalist conjecture is easily modified to admit comparative aesthetic evaluations. The upshot is that only some attributions of relational properties turn out to be non-aesthetic—properties like originality. What distinguishes them from properties like 'more sentimental than' is that they are properties of pictures as artefacts, not properties of pictures as visual presentations.

The reply is not decisive, however. Underlying the objection is an appeal to a point made above: namely, that the conjecture implies that an aesthetic evaluation cannot attribute a property to a picture unless that property is one that can be represented in the visual experience of a suitable observer who is capable of having visual experiences like mine and yours. Aesthetic evaluations have a restricted content: the reason why attributions of originality are not aesthetic is that human visual experience cannot represent pictures as original. Maybe attributions of originality are art evaluations, but can we likewise dispose of any evaluation that seems aesthetic and involves the attribution of an invisible property?

Is the question a pressing one? It is impossible to say without back-up from a theory of the contents of vision (the same goes for the analogous question, raised in Chapter 2, about seeing expressions of emotion). Such a theory does not exist. Anybody who plans one might think about its implications for accounts of pictorial expression and aesthetic evaluation.

This much can be said at least. Nothing in the internalist conjecture compels an overly narrow construal of what can enter the experience of the suitable observer and by what means. Her eye need not be 'innocent': what it represents may rely thoroughly on general background belief as well as belief specifically relevant to understanding the picture that is up for evaluation. Kendall Walton (1970) showed that evaluation is category-relative: it is one thing to find a Giorgione graceful, and another to find a Matisse graceful. It does not follow that gracefulness cannot be seen in the pictures; evaluative seeing may be category-bound.

One worry is that the internalist conjecture excludes some genuine aesthetic evaluations. A second worry is that it excludes all genuine aesthetic evaluations.

Part of what it is for the delicacy of *Woman Holding a Balance* to be a merit in it is that a suitable observer see its delicacy, and part of what it is for the sentimentality of *Moonlit Kittens* to be a demerit in it is that a suitable observer sees its sentimentality. The merit of delicacy and the demerit of sentimentality are response-dependent. But if aesthetic values are in fact response-independent, then the conjecture suffers massive extensional breakdown.

Although the conjecture implies that aesthetic values are response-dependent, nobody has seriously argued otherwise. Many argue that aesthetic properties are response-dependent (Pettit 1983; Eaton 1994; Levinson 1994; Goldman 1995*a*; Zangwill 2001), and if aesthetic properties are response-dependent, then it is natural to add that aesthetic values are too. Having said this, the conjecture is not even committed to the response-dependence of aesthetic properties. It is possible that the delicacy of *Woman Holding a Balance* is response-independent, while the fact that its being delicate is a merit in the painting is response-dependent.

That many philosophers accept the response-dependence of aesthetic properties and hence aesthetic values is no argument. Still, it is worth stressing that there is little reason to motivate opposition.

The main motivation for resisting any implication that aesthetic values are response-dependent is a worry that it leads directly to the view that aesthetic evaluations are subjective. In fact, the conjecture is consistent both with the view that aesthetic evaluations are subjective and with the contrary view that they are objective.

A representation is objective if its truth is independent of the mental condition of any particular person. Thus objectivity grounds a distinction between how things appear to a particular observer and how they are. My judgement that *Kittens* is sentimental is objective if it can be mistaken. It can be mistaken because a suitable observer would not see *Kittens* as sentimental. (Instead, she detects a clever satire of calendar kitsch.)

There are a variety of objectivist positions on aesthetic evaluation, and they can be distinguished by how they characterize the suitable observer. The suitable observer could be an ideal observer endowed with perfect knowledge and impartiality, wide experience, and fine discrimination abilities. She could be an impartial normal observer whose cognitive attributes and experience reflect the human norm (Pettit 1983). She could follow a procedural standard by which aesthetic evaluations 'admit testing by anyone who cares to take the trouble' according to 'determinate confirmation procedures that can be sketched in advance' (Mothersill 1984: 164). In all cases, the suitable observer is best understood as a hypothetical creature. So long as she would experience *Kittens* as sentimental, nobody need actually experience it as sentimental in order for its being sentimental to be a flaw that it has.

The conjecture is also consistent with the view that aesthetic evaluations are subjective. A representation is subjective if and only if its truth depends on the mental condition of the person who has or asserts the representation, so as to allow no distinction between how things appear to the person and how they are. Thus it says something about the person who has the representation rather than the object represented. In effect, an aesthetic evaluation is subjective just in case the person making the evaluation always counts as the suitable observer.

The conjecture takes no sides in the dispute over the objectivity of aesthetic evaluations. Parties to the dispute disagree about who counts as a suitable observer, which the conjecture leaves undefined. The conjecture provides a framework for thinking about the dispute. If you side with the subjectivists, you will accept that aesthetic values are response-dependent. If you side with the objectivists, you need not be troubled by the implication of response-dependence.

The implication of response-dependence is not trivial, however. It must be rejected by a super-objectivist who holds that '*Kittens* is sentimental' is a true aesthetic evaluation even if is impossible for anybody to experience it as sentimental. That is a very strong position. What facts about aesthetic response and critical discourse might it be invoked to explain?

The conjecture is formulated on the assumption that aesthetic evaluations are truth-apt, that merits such as accrue to a picture for being delicate and demerits such as accrue to a picture for being sentimental are properties of pictures. Non-cognitivists deny that there are any such properties (Bender 1996). The arguments for this position require that aesthetic evaluations be subjective and response-dependent. Since the conjecture meets this requirement, it may be possible to refit it in non-cognitivist dress. The first step is to excise the accuracy clause. Subsequent steps, should they prove necessary, are best left to interested non-cognitivists.

Not the whole aesthetic enchilada

The internalist conjecture will not settle all debates about aesthetic value, aesthetic experience, aesthetic pleasure, aesthetic concepts, and aesthetic properties. This is to its advantage. The debates are not close to resolution, so their partisans need not view the conjecture as a threat. At best, the conjecture provides a framework for continued research.

Although the second clause of the internalist conjecture has an empiricist flavour, the conjecture takes no stand on aesthetic empiricism. As we saw, aesthetic empiricism is the view that a picture has an aesthetic (de)merit because and to the extent that an experience of the picture has some intrinsic (de)merit. Clause (2) says nothing about the value of the suitable observer's experience, so it does not imply that a picture has an aesthetic (de)merit because and to the extent that an experience of the picture has some (de)merit. An aesthetic evaluation involves seeing value, but does not imply valuable seeing.

All the same, the internalist conjecture suggests a way to argue for aesthetic empiricism. Why is clause (2) true? Perhaps the best explanation of why an experience of *Kittens* as sentimental makes its sentimentality a flaw in it is that the experience of *Kittens* as sentimental is intrinsically bad. By the same token, one may accept the conjecture and reject aesthetic empiricism by denying that the latter explains the former.

The source of aesthetic value is a deep question. The conjecture suggests a way to frame it. Why is a certain experience of a suitable observer, whoever she is, part of what makes properties of works merits and demerits? Aesthetic empiricism and the pleasure theory have answers to this question. Seeing that this is the question to ask may inspire new answers.

The conjecture also suggests rough guide-lines for approaching other topics in aesthetics. Having an aesthetic experience may just be making an experiential aesthetic evaluation. If not, the theoretical challenge is to make clear what there is to aesthetic experience beyond experiential aesthetic evaluation. A similar challenge can be formulated for accounts of aesthetic pleasure, if it is a delimited category of pleasure, unless it is merely that pleasure which is routed through aesthetic evaluation.

This is speculation, and we should not lose sight of immediate concerns. A defence of interactionism requires a workable distinction between aesthetic and non-aesthetic evaluation, especially cognitive and moral evaluation.

In this regard, the great advantage of the internalist conjecture is that it does not assume that aesthetic and non-aesthetic concepts are disjointly enumerable. Standard aesthetic concepts may be non-aesthetic when they figure in non-aesthetic evaluations, and standardly non-aesthetic evaluative concepts may figure as aesthetic concepts when embedded in aesthetic evaluations. Put another way, the conjecture provides a non-aesthetic–aesthetic conversion mechanism. A critic denounces a painting as rude, leading us to wonder whether or not her evaluation is aesthetic. The evaluation is aesthetic if and only if, assuming it is accurate, the rudeness of the painting is a flaw in it and a suitable observer's experience of it as rude is part of what makes its rudeness a flaw in it.

It is an open question whether any concept used in non-aesthetic evaluation can be enlisted for duty in aesthetic evaluation—it is an open question whether interactionism is true. Chapters 4 and 5 consider how cognitive and moral evaluations double as aesthetic evaluations: they do so when concepts figuring in cognitive and moral evaluation are converted into aesthetic concepts figuring in aesthetic evaluation.

A Puzzle Reprised

One task of this chapter is to distinguish aesthetic evaluation from other varieties of evaluation so as to test interactionism. A second is to characterize the aesthetic evaluation of pictures *as pictures*—as vehicles for seeing-in. The puzzle of mimesis prompts us to ask how an aesthetic evaluation of a picture of a scene differs from an evaluation of the scene itself, seen face to face. Chapters 1 and 2 solved part of the puzzle by showing how seeing-in differs from seeing face to face. Next in line is how this difference figures in aesthetic evaluation.

Formalism

'Formalism' has many meanings. According to one usage, the term denotes a class of views which either deny or diminish the relevance of seeing-in to aesthetic evaluation, by restricting the features that are relevant to aesthetic evaluations of pictures as pictures to 'formal' features. Formalism is toothless, of course, unless something is said to distinguish those features of pictures that count as formal from those implicated in seeing-in; it is tendentious unless an argument is given to show why only formal features are relevant to aesthetic evaluations of pictures as pictures. As it turns out, the quality of the arguments for formalism depend on the conception of formal properties in play (see also Budd 1995: 49–61).

Since formalism comes in a variety of strengths, it is charitable and most informative to target the weakest and most viable (e.g. Clive Bell 1913; Fry 1927). All varieties centre on a distinction between 'plastic form' and 'illustrative content'. The former takes in lines, planes, shapes, volumes, distances, and colours, together with relationships between these elements, including gestalt groupings. The latter takes in properties a scene is depicted as having. So defined, the two classes of properties overlap: scenes are depicted as having formal properties.

Strong formalism comprises two theses. The first is that only formal properties are relevant to aesthetic evaluations of pictures as pictures. The second restricts formal properties to surface properties. No aesthetic evaluation of a picture as a picture may properly take account of its illustrative content. Any features a scene is depicted as having, including formal properties of the scene, are irrelevant.

Weak formalism endorses the first thesis but drops the restriction of formal properties to surface properties, admitting as relevant to aesthetic evaluation formal properties that the scene is depicted as having. The domain of plastic form is enlarged to encompass the lines, planes, shapes, volumes, distances, and colours in the depicted scene, as well as relationships among them. Much illustrative content remains non-formal—the objects and actions depicted, what they allude to or express, and what larger ideas are communicated—and these elements of illustrative content are not relevant to aesthetic evaluations of pictures as pictures.

Both varieties of formalism are consistent with interactionism. Neither gives us any reason to deny that plastic form can be evaluated cognitively, for instance. Perhaps good formal compositions improve the mind in the way that some believe Mozart's symphonies to raise IQ scores. Nor does formalism suggest any reason to doubt that cognitive evaluations of plastic form may also count as aesthetic evaluations. Saying that the handling of masses in a picture is insightful may count as both a cognitive and an aesthetic evaluation.

The long segregation of formalism from interactionism is a matter of mere historical accident rather than logical necessity— the one was often believed, mistakenly, to entail the other. Its consistency with interactionism means that formalism cannot be dismissed by committed interactionists. This fact threatens to drive a wedge between this book's first two and last three chapters.

Moreover, it is a virtue of formalism that it accounts for the aesthetic evaluation of pictures as pictures while neutralizing the puzzle of mimesis. There is no question of an evaluation of a picture of a scene merely mirroring an evaluation of a face-to-face experience of the scene, for only the former, when it is an evaluation of a picture as a picture, is an evaluation of a two-dimensional marked surface as such.

Formalism is not so obtuse as to ignore the obvious fact that pictures do sustain seeing-in. To explain the fact, a formalist need only recall the difference between design and surface and the role of recruitment in seeing the former (Chapter 1). Design properties are surface properties which ground seeing-in, and the content of seeing-in can transform design seeing—the formal properties of Picasso's *Portrait of Kahnweiler* are enriched once a face is seen in it. Seeing-in may be turned to formal ends.

Evaluating formalism

One pair of arguments for formalism rely upon superessentialism: an aesthetic evaluation of a picture as a picture is an evaluation of it *only* as regards properties necessarily possessed by pictures. The first argument is negative. Since not all pictures have non-formal illustrative content, an aesthetic evaluation of a picture is not an evaluation of it as regards its non-formal illustrative content. A positive argument begins with superessentialism, adds that all pictures do have formal properties (and depict scenes as having formal properties), and concludes that an aesthetic evaluation of a picture is properly an evaluation of it as regards its formal properties.

But why think that *only* properties essential to works in a medium are relevant to aesthetic evaluations of them? A sense of humour is not essential to being a teacher (even a good teacher), but having a sense of humour is sometimes a merit in a teacher, evaluated as a teacher. Likewise, pictures need not express unfamiliar emotions, but a picture's doing so may count as a merit in it when it is evaluated as a picture.

Contrast superessentialism with essentialism. According to essentialism, to evaluate a member of a kind K as a K is at least in part to evaluate it with respect to a property necessarily possessed by members of K. That is, *part* of evaluating a picture as a picture is evaluating it with respect to an essential property of pictures. Superessentialism is much stronger: *all there is* to evaluating a picture as a picture is evaluating it with respect to an essential property of pictures. Repudiating the first pair of arguments for formalism does not undercut essentialism, and it is hard to see why essentialism is not enough.

A second pair of arguments rely on exclusion: an aesthetic evaluation of a picture as a picture is properly an evaluation of it as regards properties of a kind *only* possessed by pictures (e.g. Greenberg 1961; cf. Carroll 1985). The idea is that to evaluate a work as belonging to a kind is to evaluate it as regards properties unique to members of the kind. The positive argument that springs from this assumption is that only the formal properties of their two-dimensional surfaces and designs are unique to pictures, so only those formal properties are relevant to aesthetic evaluations of them as pictures. The negative argument is that the non-formal properties which a scene is depicted as having are not unique to pictures; so, given exclusion, these properties are not relevant to aesthetic evaluation.

Both arguments are troubling in ways that point out why we should admit that non-formal illustrative content is relevant to the aesthetic evaluation of pictures as pictures.

To begin with the positive argument, the formal properties of pictures' surfaces are not unique to them—they are also found in some non-pictorial graphic works. Consider, for example, the formal properties of the page layout of some printed modern poetry (not concrete or visual poetry, which is arguably pictorial). What distinguishes a Matisse from the first issue of *Blast* is nothing formal, but rather the fact that whereas the Matisse sustains seeing-in, we see nothing in *Blast*. Far from upholding it, exclusion undermines formalism.

Weak formalism is an attractive position—many serious thinkers have espoused it—and it derives much of its attraction from the puzzle of mimesis. After all, the non-formal properties that a scene is depicted as having are not unique to pictures if the same properties are represented in face-to-face experiences of the scene. The negative argument is inspired by the desire to solve the puzzle of mimesis.

One problem with the negative argument is that it promotes strong formalism: when the *formal* properties that a scene is depicted as having are ones it could be seen to have face to face, then they are not specifically pictorial and so are not relevant to aesthetic evaluation. Setting this aside, the negative argument entails an illusionistic conception of illustrative content. (To be fair, it is a conception that formalists inherit from their non-formalist forebears.)

Sometimes seeing-in is illusionistic and divides from design seeing. In these cases, seeing scenes as having three-dimensional properties that the scenes could be seen to have face to face rules out simultaneously seeing the pictures' two-dimensional designs. However, seeing-in is not often illusionistic. Features of the design may inflect illustrative content, so that the scene is experienced as having properties it could only be seen to have in pictures. The lesson is that it is wrong to think that illustrative content is not distinctively pictorial. The negative argument from medium specificity embodies too narrow a conception of seeing-in. A distinctive feature of the medium is its affording seeing-in.

The formalist arguments from exclusion fail on their own terms.

A final argument, which eschews appeals to superessentialism and exclusion, supports only a formalism of the weakest variety yet (Fry 1927). According to this weakest formalism, an aesthetic evaluation that is grounded in a picture's illustrative content is an aesthetic evaluation of the picture as a picture, but aesthetic evaluations of a picture as illustrative and as formal arrangements are independent.

Fry's defence of this weakest formalism is also rooted in a conception of seeing-in. Evaluation of a picture as a formal composition is independent of any evaluation of it as illustrative, because we cannot simultaneously experience design and illustrative content—we must 'constantly shift attention backwards and forwards from one to the other' (Fry 1927: 23). The evaluations are independent, because the seeing with which each is concerned is divided from the other.

Like its cousins, this argument mischaracterizes seeing-in: some pictures do double seeing-in with design seeing. But it is also puzzling why divided seeing, in the case of pictures that compel it, should be thought to support the independence of formal and illustrative evaluations.

Cases of double seeing suggest that seeing formal surface features may be bound up with seeing features of the depicted scene. For instance, noticing the formal arrangement of a design may be inseparable from seeing the direction of a figure's gaze or their pointing gesture. Fry is committed to denying this possibility as inconsistent with formalism. Why? The same cross-over effects may occur when seeing is divided. What we see when we see the depicted scene alone may guide what is seen when seeing the design alone. A person suffering from a kind of visual agnosia depriving him of the ability to recognize objects, but leaving intact the ability to see colours, lines, and shapes, could not see all the formal surface properties of some pictures that promote divided seeing.

Formalism is plausible only supposing that experiences of depicted scenes are illusionistic or that aesthetic evaluations of pictures as pictures concern only their common or unique features. These suppositions are untenable. An aesthetic evaluation of a picture as a picture may legitimately take into account not only features of its design but also features of the depicted scene and the relationship between features of scene and design, seen simultaneously or in sequence. To evaluate a picture as a picture is to evaluate it as a tool for seeing-in, where seeing-in is a multi-faceted phenomenon.

Lessing's lesson

A picture is evaluated as a picture when it is evaluated as a tool for seeing-in. Gotthold Lessing famously advanced a strong version of this claim. For Lessing, the beauty of a picture lies in its depiction of something as beautiful. No beautiful picture may depict a scene as on the whole ugly or repulsive; a picture's depicting a scene as ugly or repulsive makes the picture itself repulsive on the whole (Lessing 1962; see Savile 1987: 3–20). The falsity of Lessing's strong claim explains resistance to mimeticism. A weaker claim preserves a grain of truth from Lessing and softens resistance to mimeticism.

In fact, Lessing's view comprises two claims that are better distinguished. One is that the aesthetic merits and demerits of pictures transmit or reflect those of the scenes they depict. The second is that aesthetic merit is beauty and demerit ugliness.

The spirit of the first claim may be preserved while dropping the second claim identifying aesthetic merit with beauty. One might assert that being F is an aesthetic merit in a picture if and only if the picture depicts a scene as F and being F is an aesthetic merit *in the scene.* (Being F is an aesthetic demerit in a picture if and only if the picture depicts a scene as F and being F is an aesthetic demerit in the scene.) Thus may beauty be an aesthetic flaw in a Francis Bacon portrait: it depicts a scene as beautiful, and that is a merit in the scene but not, in this case, in the depiction of it.

Even so weakened, this version of mimeticism is too strong. First, it denies outright that a picture's surface properties are relevant to its aesthetic evaluation. An arrangement of shapes on the picture surface may be dynamic or energetic, and this may be a merit in the work, though the shapes are not ones the scene is depicted as having. Second, it denies the possibility that a merit in a picture may be a demerit in the object depicted, and a demerit in a picture may be a merit in the object depicted. The Bacon is repulsive in so far as it depicts an object as repulsive; yet, while the object's depicted repulsiveness is a demerit in the object, the picture's repulsiveness is meritorious. Meritorious depiction does not entail, and is not entailed by, merit in what is depicted.

Our latter-day Lessing may spurn intuition and embrace the consequences of her account, insisting that formal surface properties are not relevant to aesthetic evaluations of pictures as pictures and that aesthetic merit in a picture is determined by the aesthetic merit of objects in the depicted scene. She would be reasonable in accepting these consequences if moved by arguments for mimeticism.

However, Lessing's arguments prefigure the formalists' super-essentialist and exclusionist arguments. Pictures, Lessing argues, are properly evaluated as pictures only when they are evaluated with respect either to properties common to all pictures or specific only to pictures, and all pictures and only pictures sustain object-presenting experiences of scenes. The trouble is that these arguments depend on a distorted conception of seeing-in. Our intuitions run contrary to the consequences of strong mimeticism, because we have an intuitive grasp of how surface and design seeing comport with seeing-in.

Mimetic merit

Not all evaluations of pictures are aesthetic, and not all evaluate pictures *as pictures*; but some evaluations of pictures as pictures are aesthetic. According to essentialism, to evaluate a picture as a picture is to evaluate it, at least in part, with respect to a property necessarily possessed by pictures. Since pictures are necessarily vehicles for seeing-in, an evaluation of a picture as a picture is an evaluation of it as a vehicle for seeing-in. The same goes for aesthetic evaluations of pictures as pictures. To see this, consider how seeing-in may figure in the internalist conjecture.

The intricacies of the conjecture can be distracting; a useful and harmless simplification restricts it to

basic aesthetic evaluation: a suitable observer's accurate evaluative experience, E, of P as F is a basic aesthetic evaluation of P as a picture if and only if (1) being F is a (de)merit in P and (2) E is partly constitutive of (1).

In basic cases, aesthetic evaluations are accurate experiences of suitable observers. Suppose you are a suitable observer and you accurately experience Seurat's *Grand Jatte* as aloof. Your experience is an aesthetic evaluation if its aloofness is a demerit in it and your experience of it as aloof is part of what makes its being aloof a flaw.

An evaluation of a picture is aesthetic only if it is a visual experience of the picture. It is an evaluation of a picture as a picture only if the experience involves seeing-in. The involvement may be direct or indirect.

Take the indirect case first. Suppose that an experience of Spiegelman's drawing in Figure 10 as chilling is an accurate aesthetic evaluation of it. If it is chilling, it is chilling in large measure because of what is to be seen in it: a world structured by an ideology of hate. The experience of the picture as chilling is explained by what is expressed by the scene it depicts, and that is explained in turn by what is to be seen in the picture (see Chapter 2). The rule for indirect cases is that

a suitable observer's accurate evaluative experience, E, of P as F is a basic aesthetic evaluation of P as a picture because (1) being F is a (de)merit in P, (2) E is partly constitutive of (1), and (3) P is experienced as F because O is seen as G in P.

The experience of the panel from *Maus* as chilling is an aesthetic evaluation because being chilling is a merit in it, its being seen as chilling is part of what makes its being chilling a merit in it, and because seeing it as chilling is a consequence of seeing in it a world upon which a swastika is inscribed.

When involvement is direct, the suitable observer's experience just is an experience of seeing-in. In general,

an experience, E, of seeing O as F in P is a basic aesthetic evaluation of P as a picture because (1) seeing O as F in P is a (de)merit in P and (2) E is partly constitutive of (1).

Since experience is transitive, the experience of seeing O as F in P just is seeing O as F in P; so in direct cases, seeing-in is a type of evaluation. The setting in which Vermeer's woman weighs her goods is serene, and 'serene' appears on Sibley's list of aesthetic terms. Your experience of seeing the room as serene in the painting is a basic aesthetic evaluation because it is a merit in it that you see in it a serene space, and your so seeing it is part of what makes it a merit in the painting that it sustains seeing the room as serene.

Seeing-in is essentially involved, whether directly or indirectly, in aesthetic evaluations of pictures as pictures. These evaluations are not merely aesthetic evaluations of pictures in which we see things. They are aesthetic evaluations of pictures for their sustaining our seeing things in them. The experience that is partly constitutive of value is or is explained by an experience of seeing-in.

If Chapter 1 is roughly correct, then there are several species of seeing-in, each distinguished by how it stands in relation to design seeing (Table 1). In some pictures seeing-in doubles with design seeing, with the result that one sees the design as undergirding the depicted scene. In other pictures, seeing-in divides from design seeing (but not surface seeing), and it is necessary to switch between seeing scene and design. When seeing-in divides from surface seeing, the result is *trompe-l'œil*: seeing O in P is phenomenally indistinguishable from seeing O face to face. Except in *trompe-l'œil*, seeing O in P is quite different phenomenally from seeing O face to face; O is

seen to have properties in P that it is not seen to have with the
naked eye.

This taxonomy of the species of seeing-in is a simplification,
however, since it only admits of pure cases. Most pictures *trompe-
l'œil* with respect to some properties, double seeing-in and design
seeing with regard to other properties, and divide seeing-in from
design seeing with regard to a third set of properties. These are
impure cases. The distinction between pure and impure cases
means that the variety of seeing-in is manifest inter-pictorially and
also intra-pictorially.

The shadows cast by the coffers adorning the dome in Figure 6
are an example of *trompe-l'œil*. On the surface of van Gogh's painting
of a pair of boots (Fig. 3), we see caked-on paint; at the same time we
see the boots in the painting as caked in mud. Seeing the caked-on
paint doubles with seeing the caked-on mud. We see how the
former underlies the latter. Vermeer is justly renowned for his
ability to capture intense points of light. The pearls and the pans of
the balance in *Woman Holding a Balance* (Fig. 1) seem not so much
to reflect ambient light as to radiate it from within. Seeing the
brightness of the pearls in the picture blocks seeing the dabs of
white paint in virtue of which the points of light are depicted.
Seeing-in divides from design seeing, but there is no *trompe-l'œil*.

Any kind of seeing-in may be involved directly or indirectly in a
basic aesthetic evaluation. The Vermeer is vivid, and that is partly
because precisely bounded pin-points of light are to be seen in it,
and the light seems not to have a source in the paint. The van Gogh
is earthy in part because we see mud-caked boots in it and equally
see the paint that renders the mud as caked on the canvas like mud.

Pictures promote seeing-in, but seeing-in is a multifaceted
phenomenon. An aesthetic evaluation of a picture as a picture
evaluates it as a vehicle for one or more varieties of seeing-in. This
is the essential power and appeal of pictures.

4   DRAWING LESSONS

How can one learn the truth by thinking? As one learns to see a face better by drawing it.

Ludwig Wittgenstein

Many representations are cognitive tools: they extend the power of thought. Historical chronicles extend human memory, for instance, and written proofs in logic extend the power of reasoning. Pictures also empower thinking, by showing us how things look. Recognizing people would be less reliable without portraits, surgery more precarious without anatomical drawings, and catalogue shopping a disappointing lottery without photographs. Plato's refusal to see that pictures ever have cognitive merit is among his most egregious blunders. Granting this, one might nevertheless deny that the cognitive value of pictures ever has anything to do with their aesthetic value. This chapter argues that the domains of cognitive and aesthetic evaluation are not so distantly separated. Evaluations of paintings as, for example, true to life, profound, didactic, or distorting (see Roskill and Carrier 1983) are cognitive and aesthetic.

Cognitivism

According to interactionism, there is some type of non-aesthetic evaluation, V, such that some aesthetic evaluations imply or are implied by some V-evaluations. Cognitivism is a version of interactionism according to which some aesthetic evaluations imply or are implied by some cognitive evaluations. There are several alternatives to cognitivism that arguments for it must address.

Radical cognitivism identifies aesthetic evaluation with cognitive evaluation, or a special case of it. Nelson Goodman writes that 'aesthetic experience is cognitive experience distinguished by the dominance of certain symbolic characteristics and judged by the standards of cognitive efficacy' (1976: 262). More recently, James Young has argued that the aesthetic function of artworks is cognitive, so that good artworks are those that provide valuable insight, while poor works are those that convey little of interest (1995: 65).

The polar opposite of radical cognitivism is radical anti-cognitivism. According to this view, aesthetic merit blocks cognitive merit, and vice versa. That is, any attribution of aesthetic merit implies an attribution of cognitive demerit, and any attribution of cognitive merit implies an attribution of aesthetic demerit. Those who might be called 'puritans' take a finding of aesthetic merit to establish cognitive worthlessness. Surprisingly, many contemporary artists believe that if a work is to provoke serious thought, it must be ugly, disturbing, or difficult to look at; it is mindless if it is pretty. Ironically standing shoulder to shoulder with the puritans are the 'aesthetes', who view an attribution of cognitive merit to be proof of didacticism—the ultimate aesthetic failure. They too are radical anti-cognitivists.

A more plausible contrary of cognitivism is autonomism. On this view, some pictures have both cognitive and aesthetic merit, and others have both cognitive and aesthetic demerit, but the coincidence is always fortuitous (Morgan 1953; Lamarque and Olsen 1994: 321–36). As a result, it is always a mistake to reason from an aesthetic to a cognitive evaluation, or from a cognitive to an aesthetic evaluation.

Cognitivism also holds that some pictures have both cognitive and aesthetic merit, and others have both cognitive and aesthetic demerit, but it adds that sometimes the coincidence is not accidental. What explains a picture's having one kind of (de)merit explains its having the other. It follows that some aesthetic evaluations imply or are implied by cognitive evaluations with the same valence (Hursthouse 1992; Graham 1995).

Not at issue, on any of these views, is the sceptical question as to whether pictures *ever* have cognitive merit. All disagree with Plato and agree with wedding photographers, catalogue designers, and anatomists that some pictures extend human cognition beneficially.

While this agreement is gratifying, it is also potentially misleading. The reason is that the plausibility of each position depends on what account it adopts of the cognitive value of pictures. Indeed, autonomism and cognitivism are not even contrary positions on an entirely unrestricted conception of the cognitive value of pictures. If 'cognition' is used to name such goods as experiencing, perceiving, learning, remembering, conceptualizing, interpreting, explaining, deducing, imagining, and knowing, then it is pointless to deny that aesthetic evaluation is cognitive. The collapse of autonomism into cognitivism is stopped by a refined conception of cognitive value according to which not every kind of cognitive state or activity is valuable. The same goes for any version of cognitivism that is not trivially true. An argument for cognitivism should therefore begin by adopting the right conception of pictures' cognitive value.

Knowing Pictures

One aim of inquiry is the acquisition of knowledge, and any mental operation or state has cognitive merit in so far as it either adds to what we know or increases the ratio of knowledge to non-knowledge (for sake of convenience let the former include the latter). Perception, learning, memory, and many other faculties are instruments in the acquisition, storage, and retrieval of a repository of knowledge needed to manipulate our environment, ourselves, and other people. Many artefacts have cognitive merit because they boost the power of these faculties. Many representations are artefacts of this sort; it is natural to think that pictures have cognitive merit to the extent that they contribute to knowledge.

Knowing in, through, and about

Even Plato should grant that some knowledge can be obtained from pictures.

Looking at Rembrandt's painting *Belshazzar's Feast* in the National Gallery (Fig. 11), you may learn that it is painted in oils, that there are paintings by Rembrandt in London, and that it depicts the divine hand. These are instances of 'knowledge about' a picture—knowledge about the picture's properties as a physical object, including its representational properties—for instance, that it is a divine-hand-representing-picture. We can know these facts about a picture just as we know similar facts about any object.

Since pictures are artefacts, we can infer from them facts about their makers and the historical conditions in which their

Fig. 11. Rembrandt, *Belshazzar's Feast*, c.1635. Photo credit: Art Resource, NY.

makers worked. Call knowledge of these facts 'knowledge through' a picture. Through *Belshazzar's Feast* you may come to know that Rembrandt had some grasp of Hebrew letters (not the Hebrew language), that he was influenced by the Caravaggisti, or that seventeenth-century Dutch painters believed biblical figures dressed in the manner of seventeenth-century Dutchmen. This is the same kind of knowledge as we can glean about people and their circumstances from observing their actions.

The sort of knowledge at issue in the debate between autonomism and cognitivism is 'knowledge in' pictures. One good candidate for knowledge in *Belshazzar's Feast* is, briefly stated, that it is a mistake to be dazzled by worldly pleasures at the expense of spiritual matters. That is, as one might say, the painting's 'lesson'.

The lessons that pictures are alleged to teach are ambitious. They take in scientific knowledge (e.g. Seurat's *Grande Jatte*), historical knowledge (e.g. David's *Tennis Court Oath*), and knowledge of human psychology (e.g. Rembrandt's self-portraits)—as well as knowledge of what we ought to value. Indeed, the lesson of *Belshazzar's Feast* is itself about a lesson. You, as viewer of the picture, may identify with Belshazzar by coming to see that it is a mistake to be dazzled by Rembrandt's fine handiwork, especially the stunning rendering of gold and jewels, at the expense of the picture's deeper, spiritual message. Do you learn any better than the king? One lesson of the picture is about the capacity of pictures to teach lessons.

Knowledge-about, knowledge-through, and knowledge-in are distinct because they have different kinds of contents. Of course, this does not mean that each must be sought in isolation from the others. Knowledge-in may provide clues to knowledge-through, and, with regard to modern art, whose message so often concerns art and art-making itself, a piece of knowledge-in is often knowledge-through. As a practical matter, critics and historians often draw upon all three at once (Baxandall 1985, 1988; Haskell 1993). Nevertheless, the distinctions between the three kinds of knowledge do not obliterate these complexities; they allow us to discern them.

Knowledge and warrant

All three kinds of knowledge conform to the standard, triadic account of knowledge as warranted (or justified), true belief. To know that *Belshazzar's Feast* is painted in oils requires believing that it is. Since the contents of beliefs are propositions, the content of knowledge is also propositional. Moreover, a proposition known must be true—belief in false propositions is apparent knowledge at best. (The required notion of truth is the minimal 'semantic' conception according to which 'Rembrandt painted in oils' is true if and only if Rembrandt painted in oils.)

Knowledge, on the standard, triadic account, requires more than true belief, for true beliefs acquired by guessing or by out-and-out faulty reasoning are not known. To count as knowledge, a belief must be warranted. A belief's warrant consists in its conforming to a set of norms whose goals are the accumulation of true beliefs and the avoidance of false ones. Since guessing is a poor way to acquire true beliefs and a good way to acquire erroneous ones, a belief, even one that is true, lacks warrant if it is acquired by guessing.

There is considerable contention about the norms to which warranted beliefs conform. Some hold that a belief's warrant is a matter of the quality of the reasons or evidence a believer has for her belief. Others hold that a belief's warrant is a matter of the reliability of the process by which the belief is formed, where more reliable processes are just those more likely to generate true beliefs.

We need take no position on theories of warrant. If it turns out that, on a given theory of warrant, pictures are not sources of knowledge, then that is a good reason to prefer a competing theory of warrant. After all, the task of a theory of warrant is to explain part of what is involved in our knowing what we know. Only if pictures fail to convey knowledge on *any* plausible theory of warrant should we question whether pictures convey knowledge at all.

The pieces of knowledge extracted from *Belshazzar's Feast* illustrate the variety of grounds that can warrant knowledge about and through pictures. The belief that the painting is executed in oils

may be warranted simply in virtue of the fact that it derives from
your seeing that it is painted in oils. The belief that Rembrandt
borrowed from some of the Caravaggisti is warranted on the basis of
more extensive evidence, including facts about what the picture
depicts, the look of pictures by ter Brugghen, the likelihood that
Rembrandt was familiar with ter Brugghen's work, the prevalence of
the practice of borrowing in European painting, and the small
chance that Rembrandt would have painted his picture as he did
were he not familiar with ter Brugghen's work.

The relationship of knowledge-through to its warranting grounds
is typically that of inference to the best explanation. If pictures like
Belshazzar's Feast are the sole evidence in its favour, the belief that
seventeenth-century Dutch painters thought that biblical figures
dressed in the manner of seventeenth-century Dutchmen is unwarranted. That this is how Rembrandt and his contemporaries
depicted biblical figures offers little evidence for the claim that they
were unaware of the anachronism unless competing explanations
are excluded. For instance, biblical figures may have been put
in contemporary dress in order to decrease the viewer's sense of
distance from the events portrayed, and thus to give religious stories
a contemporary relevance.

This brief sketch of the elements of knowledge about and
knowledge through pictures is far too coarse a net to catch many
complex and subtle questions that may be asked about the basis,
status, and proper methods of art-historical and art-critical inquiry.
It does, however, set a rough benchmark for knowledge in
pictures—a benchmark that loose talk about knowledge in pictures
fails to clear.

Statements blue or green

How can pictures convey knowledge-in if the contents of knowledge
are propositions? As Gombrich remarks, 'a picture can no more be
true or false than a statement can be blue or green' (1961: 59). There

is something to be said for this. A still life by Chardin depicts a collection of objects as appearing a certain way, and a grasp of the picture requires only that its viewer see the objects in it; but seeing-in is arguably non-propositional—grant Gombrich the point that it is. On the other side, it seems that pictures do engender beliefs. I do not commit a gross conceptual blunder by undertaking to interpret *Belshazzar's Feast* as evincing certain claims, as I would were I to search the text of *Emma* for an object-presenting experience of its title character. The knowledge theory of pictures' cognitive merit depends on sorting this out.

Statements are not blue or green; pictures are not true or false. After all, statements are actions asserting propositions, and actions have no colours, whereas only propositions are true or false, and pictures are not propositions. Accepting these platitudes leaves room to claim that persons can make statements by making or displaying pictures (Novitz 1977; Eaton 1980). To take a historical example, Dorothea Lange exhibited *Migrant Mother* in order to assert that we ought to help the poor, who are noble and do not deserve their poverty (Fig. 12). We need not say that the photograph makes this claim, but rather that Lange makes the claim by making and displaying a photograph that depicts what it does.

This is consistent with Gombrich's observation that pictures do not express propositions. Indeed, what a statement asserts is not always the proposition expressed by the sentence used in making the assertion. What a speaker means by her utterance and what the sentence uttered means are not always identical. In saying 'The black flies are a torment', I may be asserting that the mosquitoes are a torment (I have a poor grasp of entomology). Pictures and sentences are not so far apart, then. People make pictures in order to assert propositions that are not part of the pictures' contents, just as they speak sentences to assert propositions that are not part of the sentences' contents.

However, what a sentence is normally used to assert is the proposition that the sentence expresses. The sentence 'It is raining' expresses the proposition that it is raining, and for this reason it is

Fig. 12. Dorothea Lange, *Migrant Mother*, 1936. Photo Credit: Digital Image © The Museum of Modern Art/Licensed by SCALA/Art Resource, NY.

apt for use in assertions that it is raining. By contrast, since pictures are non-propositional, what a picture is apt to assert cannot be identified with a proposition it expresses. Yet surely the content of a picture somehow constrains what it may appropriately be used to assert. How so?

Call the contents of perceptual beliefs 'perceptual reports'. Perceptual reports of a scene are those propositions about objects in a perceived scene that would be true were the experience of the scene accurate. Likewise, 'pictorial reports' of a depicted scene are propositions about objects in the scene that would be true were the picture accurate. Perhaps, then, a picture is apt for the assertion of those propositions that are pictorial reports of the scene it depicts.

This proposal is both too broad and too narrow. It is too broad because most pictures have an indefinite number of pictorial reports, most of which they are not apt to assert. If *Belshazzar's Feast* is accurate, gold is yellow in colour, but the painting is not a treatise on the metals. Moreover, a picture may be used to make a true statement even though most (maybe all) of the pictorial reports associated with it are false (Korsmeyer 1985). Paul Revere's broadsheet illustration of the Boston Massacre is apt to assert, truly, that the event occurred by moonlight, though it wrongly depicts the moon as waxing. The reply, of course, is that the detail is irrelevant. The contents of pictures may be needlessly and inaccurately determinate. However, this reply reinforces the worry that pictorial reports fail to constrain what pictures may be used to assert.

The proposal is too narrow because pictures can be used to assert propositions not found among their pictorial reports. *Migrant Mother* represents its subject as having many properties, but it does not represent your relationship to her, so it is not among its pictorial reports that you ought to help those who need aid through no fault of their own.

In sum, the message that *Migrant Mother* is apt to assert depends on its pictorial content, but the dependence is not explicable in terms of the dependence of pictorial report upon pictorial content.

Assertion is an action like any other. Just as a reasonable determination of what a person is doing is a hypothesis that explains his or her movements, so a reasonable interpretation of what a person is making a picture to assert is a hypothesis that explains his or her endowing a picture with the content it has. The remarkable detail in the lines of the face of the migrant mother, the quiet pride and determination she expresses, and the depiction of the children with their backs to the viewer, not only add up to a powerful image, but also give us reason to interpret it as an appropriate vehicle for Lange's message. The suggestion is that a picture is apt to assert that p if and only if the hypothesis that the picture is apt to assert p best explains the picture's having the content it has.

In the background is the assumption that some pictures are made to have contents that make them apt for use in asserting certain propositions and not others. The assumption is reasonable if pictures are made so as to conform to communicative norms, such as H. P. Grice's maxims of conversational implicature. Amongst the maxims are: make your statement as informative as is required but no more informative than is required; do not say what you believe is false or unwarranted; be relevant; avoid obscurity and ambiguity; be brief and be orderly (Grice 1975: 67). An interpretation explains a picture's content on the assumption that it is geared towards effective communication.

(Interpretation may also take into account a work's larger communicative context, including the historical context in which it was made, traditions and conventions of genre and style, influences on its maker, and the shape of the maker's *œuvre*. For example, one fact relevant to interpreting Rembrandt's *Belshazzar's Feast* is its departure from the scriptural story: whereas the story describes the king as submitting in terror, Rembrandt depicts him as defiantly guarding his treasure.)

The limits of warrant

Migrant Mother is apt to assert that we ought to act with greater compassion for the poor. Are propositions such as this the kinds of propositions that we can come to know by looking at the pictures used to assert them? Some pictures are certainly used to assert true propositions. Are we ever warranted in believing them? If not, then why think that pictures have a cognitive value any greater than a lucky guess? If so, then what is the source of warrant for knowledge in pictures?

It is convenient to use 'warrant schemas' to represent the warranting grounds for beliefs, if they are warranted. Here is a warrant schema for my perceptual belief that the notebook on the table before me is black.

1. I see the notebook as black.
2. I am a normally equipped observer in normal viewing conditions.
3. Perceptual reports of normally equipped observers in normal viewing conditions have a high probability of being true.

Except for externalists, the truth of these claims does not suffice to warrant perceptual belief. Internalists add that a belief is warranted only if the believer has cognitive access to its warranting grounds in the form of reasons. The warrant schema merely lists the grounds warranting a belief while remaining neutral on whether the believer must have access to them as reasons.

There are two candidates for the grounds warranting knowing in a picture. Warrant may be located either in a picture's content and its reports or in facts about its creation.

The former can be modelled on the warrant schema of perceptual beliefs (Young 1996: 257–8). Thus my belief that Gertrude is formidable may be warranted by grounds such as these:

1. In the picture I see Gertrude as formidable.
2. So the picture reports that Gertrude is formidable.
3. Pictorial reports have a high probability of being true.

This identifies the contents of knowledge-in with pictorial reports, and we have seen that identification is inadequate. Set that aside. More seriously, (3) is obviously false. Pictures can and very often do misrepresent; their reports are often wrong.

Some classes of pictures are reliably accurate—because they are made in a certain way (Cohen and Meskin 2004). As a result, facts about the making of a picture ground warrant. Take photography as a case in point.

1. Nigel sees in the picture Elvis living in Winnipeg.
2. So the picture reports that Elvis lives in Winnipeg.

3. The picture is made by a photographic process.
4. Pictorial reports of pictures made photographically have a high
   probability of being true.

Such grounds warrant Nigel's pictorially derived belief that Elvis is
living in Winnipeg. Granted, photographs can be doctored, but
the schema does not require that photographs never misrepresent:
warrant does not ensure certainty.

The same goes for pictures that serve as vehicles for what might
be considered a pictorial form of testimony.

1. Turner sees in the drawing the epitrochoidal shape of a rotary
   engine housing.
2. So the drawing reports that rotary engine housings are
   epitrochoidal.
3. The drawing is displayed on howstuffworks.com.
4. Pictorial reports of drawings displayed on howstuffworks.com
   have a high probability of being true.

These grounds warrant the belief that the housing of rotary
engines has the shape of an epitrochoid. A great deal of what we
know is warranted because we have it from an expert or a reliable
witness, and pictures can transmit expert and testimonial knowledge. Some picture-creators who make statements through their
pictures have a high probability of being correct, so we are warranted in believing them.

Knowledge-in can be obtained from some pictures. However,
this is not yet proof of cognitivism. Autonomists may accept that
pictures have cognitive value in so far as they convey knowledge-in,
yet deny that the merit of conveying knowledge-in implies any
aesthetic merit.

Appeal to the internalist conjecture supports the autonomists'
take on the matter. Suppose a picture is accurately evaluated as
conveying a truth. The evaluation is a cognitive one. It implies
an aesthetic one only if the merit of its conveying a truth is partly
constituted by a suitable observer's seeing it as conveying the truth.

It is hard to see how that condition could be met. That a representation conveys a truth is a merit in it independent of any response to it. If the merit is independent of the response, it does not imply any evaluation that requires the response. So it does not imply an aesthetic evaluation. The same goes for evaluations of a picture as warranting a claim.

The cognitivist may reply that some aesthetic evaluations of pictures imply evaluations of warrant or truthfulness. The message of *Migrant Mother* owes a great deal to its aesthetic aspects—from its composition, lighting, and printing to the fine balance it strikes between the depiction of pride and resourcefulness on the one hand and despair and vulnerability on the other. However, these have everything to do with the persuasive power of the image and nothing to do with the truthfulness or warrant of its message. A photograph much like *Migrant Mother* that is an aesthetic disaster would be less persuasive but as true, and it would give us equal reason to believe that we ought to help the needy. Persuasiveness is not warrant: effectiveness at converting belief is not having warrant for belief.

Peter Lamarque and Stein Haugom Olsen observe that in literary criticism,

> there is an absence of argument about whether or not a particular proposition or set of propositions implied in a literary work is true or false. Indeed, critical work is ended when it has been demonstrated how such a general proposition or set of propositions organizes the various features of the work into a meaningful pattern. (1994: 332).

Likewise, criticism of pictures is never concerned with the quality of the warranting grounds that pictures supply for the claims they are used to make—critics do not weigh the quality of evidence which *Belshazzar's Feast* offers for its religious message. They are concerned with persuasiveness, however. *Migrant Mother* quite effectively inspires acceptance, and it is part of criticism to take note of this, though it is no part of criticism to point out that the photograph draws a generalization from an inadequate sample.

Pictures have cognitive value—that is undisputed. The dispute centres on whether findings of cognitive (de)merit in pictures ever imply or are implied by findings of aesthetic (de)merit. How the dispute is resolved depends on what the cognitive value of pictures is taken to be. The prospects for cognitivism look gloomy if pictures have cognitive merit only in so far as they convey knowledge.

Beyond truth and warrant

One might grumble that the knowledge-in account is a caricature of what philosophers have in mind when they say that pictures and other artistic representations convey knowledge. It is not propositional knowledge amenable to analysis by the standard, triadic account of knowledge. It is a different creature entirely.

Nobody has managed a remotely clear description of the creature (e.g. Hospers 1946; Reid 1980; Beardsley 1981: 374–9). Dorothy Walsh unhelpfully characterizes it as 'knowing beyond saying' (1969: 104). Rosalind Hursthouse writes that it is 'immensely complicated and subtle, expressed more readily in action and reaction than summed up in mere statements, embodied in particulars rather than in abstractions' (1992: 295–6). This is hardly firm ground on which to build an argument for cognitivism.

That granted, it is too soon to capitulate. The standard, triadic account of knowledge-in performs the following service, at a minimum. It indicates what is left over when we see why knowing in pictures, though valuable, fails to meet the needs of cognitivism. What is missing is a role for experience.

Virtuous Vision

The language of cognitive evaluation targets traits as well as states (of belief). Persons are praised as insightful, curious, open-minded, clear, determined, impartial, or thorough. They are also denounced as obtuse, complacent, narrow, confused, pig-headed, biased, or lazy. We achieve at least some of our cognitive goals through the exercise of several 'intellectual virtues', and the possession of an intellectual virtue is, all things considered, a cognitive good (e.g. Kornblith 1983; Code 1987; Sosa 1991; Hookway 1994; Zagzebski 1996). Perhaps pictures have cognitive value in so far as they contribute to the development of some intellectual virtues or vices.

Intellectual virtue

An intellectual virtue is, first, a relatively enduring and entrenched trait of a thinker. The trait is acquired, generally as a consequence of some effort, and it can be lost, through effort or accidentally.

Second, the trait is a disposition to achieve some cognitive goal. The goal may be to form true beliefs or knowledge, but we may not wish to rule out other cognitive goals, such as understanding or mere relief from agnosticism (Hookway 1994: 223). The key point is that 'virtue' is a success concept and a degree concept: to have an intellectual virtue is to enjoy, in ordinary circumstances, a high measure of success in achieving a cognitive goal. Moreover, this success can be no accident: it is due in part to the disposition's being part of a person's cognitive equipment.

Externalists hold that the possession of an entrenched disposition to reliable success in achieving a cognitive goal is sufficient for intellectual virtue (Sosa 1991). If it is a virtue to have the courage of one's convictions, then a person possesses the virtue when they stand by their beliefs in a way that is reliably conducive to truth or some other cognitive goal.

Internalists hold that intellectual virtue has a third component, though there is no agreement about what it is (Kornblith 1983; Code 1987; Zagzebski 1996). To take one account as an example, Linda Zagzebski argues that an intellectual virtue has a motivational component (1996: 132–7). A motive, according to Zagzebski, is an action-guiding emotion, and a motivation is a tendency to act in certain circumstances from certain motives. Intellectual courage, for example, is a tendency to be moved by confidence in one's beliefs so as to reliably achieve a cognitive goal. This means that acquiring an intellectual virtue has two parts: one must develop the appropriate motivations, and one must also become better at achieving the relevant cognitive goal by acting as one is motivated. One may lose an intellectual virtue either by losing the appropriate motivation or by becoming unreliable at achieving one's cognitive goals.

Israel Scheffler's (1991) discussion of the cognitive emotions sheds some light on the motivational component of intellectual virtue. A cognitive emotion is one whose intentional object is the epistemic status of the subject's beliefs, experiences, predictions, or expectations. Joy at verification is experienced when a person uses a theory to make a prediction and finds the prediction verified. What characterizes the emotion is its intentional object, the belief that what has happened is what was predicted—against a background expectation that one's predictions are not always correct. Another cognitive emotion is surprise, whose intentional object is a recognition that what has happened conflicts with expectation. Both surprise and joy at verification require a healthy sense of fallibility, on the one hand, and a willingness to be open to the revision of one's expectations, on the other. Scheffler writes that, 'to the extent that we are capable of surprise, the possibility that our expectations are wrong is alive for us, and thus our joy in verification, if it occurs, is not utterly deluded. Receptive to surprise, we are capable of learning from experience' (1991: 12).

There is no pressing reason to take a stand on the debate between externalists and internalists. Externalists grant that intellectual virtues may include a motivation (though they need not) and so are free to accept that pictures do instil a motivation to cognitive action. They deny only that pictures must instil such a motivation if they are to be credited with fostering an intellectual virtue.

A final caveat. Some hope to derive an account of warrant from an account of intellectual virtue, by arguing that a belief is warranted only if it issues from a virtuous belief-forming process (Sosa 1991;

Hookway 1994) or else is one that an intellectually virtuous person would believe (Zagzebski 1996). The conception of intellectual virtue required in defence of cognitivism is not one from which other epistemic concepts, such as warrant, must be derivable. Remaining non-committal about the role of intellectual virtue in an analysis of warrant allows for a more roomy conception of the virtues. The extra room is likely to come in handy for building a non-epistemic conception of pictures' cognitive merit.

Fine observation

What we do when we interpret or appreciate pictures does not always realize cognitive goals such as acquiring knowledge or maximizing true belief, but it does often depend on the exercise of intellectual virtues. An obtuse person will not get far with a still life by Chardin, and inquisitiveness is key to appreciating an allegory by Poussin or R. B. Kitaj. Likewise, it takes intellectual courage to face up to the picture of humanity realized by Goya's war drawings.

Having said that, it is one thing to require an intellectual virtue and another to foster or reinforce its development. Why not think that pictures take advantage of intellectual capacities to which they make no contribution?

The motivation to acquire a virtue may not be the very motivation that moves a person to act virtuously. If appreciating a picture depends on the exercise of an intellectual virtue, one might acquire the virtue because one wants to appreciate the work. Moreover, if one acquires an intellectual virtue by doing what a virtuous person would do, then a work may not only give one a reason to acquire the virtue but may also assist one in its acquisition. Making sense of a painting by Kitaj requires open-mindedness, so it requires a closed-minded person to become more open-minded, while also providing her with an opportunity to become more open-minded, simply by trying to do what it asks of her. Her motivation is to enjoy or just understand the picture, but by acting on it she gains a motivation to be more open-minded.

So although the intellectual virtues aim at the achievement of cognitive goals which may differ from the goals of people appreciating pictures, a picture may nevertheless have cognitive merit because it fosters or reinforces an intellectual virtue.

This is a possibility; do pictures in fact foster or reinforce some intellectual virtue? In answering this question, we may proceed in one of two ways.

One is to list the intellectual virtues, or most of them, or those about which there is likely to be little disagreement, and then see whether pictures foster or reinforce the development of the listed virtues. Sadly, our theoretical understanding of the intellectual virtues is rudimentary. Any list is likely to be tentative and incomplete. It may just as well turn out that a full understanding of the individual intellectual virtues will depend on our having ascertained what faculties pictures call to action.

The alternative procedure is first to identify the demands that pictures make of us, if we are to appreciate them fully, and then to consider whether and in what way meeting these demands requires and thereby fosters or reinforces the development of intellectual excellence. Since nothing is more important in an engagement with a picture than responsiveness to the demands of the work, the second procedure starts us in the right place.

One demand that fine pictures obviously make of us is that we be 'fine observers'. Here there is a symmetry between what is required of pictures' makers and what is required of their viewers. Drawing well requires seeing well, as does appreciating what a picture has to offer. Some scientists, such as astronomers and biologists, whose work depends upon gathering visually presented data, learn to draw well. Part of learning to draw and look at pictures is learning to see better. But what is it to 'see better'?

First, many pictures require and foster 'delicacy of discrimination', for they are dense representations in which every difference in the marking of the picture surface and every difference in the way a scene is depicted is something to notice. As Goodman put it, 'where there is density in the symbol system, familiarity is never complete and final;

another look may always disclose significant new subtleties' (1976: 260). True, some pictures are stylized or sketchy; but even these require delicacy of discrimination, because any difference in the curve of a stylized line or in the gesture of a sketchy drawing may make a significant difference.

Second, many pictures demand 'accuracy in seeing'. Some jolt us out of tired ways of seeing the familiar, so that we come to see freshly and more accurately (Gombrich 1982*b*). Oscar Wilde quipped that a change in (perception of) the climate of London was due to the Impressionists—they showed the fog to be full of colour, and we now see it as colourful. Other pictures draw attention, not to features of the objects seen, but to felt qualities of experience itself, to what it is like to see things. Illustrating this, according to Michael Baxandall, is the work of Chardin (1985: 74–104).

Third, many pictures demand 'adaptability of seeing': they enable us to see what is otherwise invisible. We never see with the naked eye objects looking as they do when we see them in cubist painting, Haida split-style painting, or engineering and architectural drawings (Chapter 1). By making the otherwise invisible visible, pictures may stretch the powers of vision. Moreover, the visual system's upgrade is not limited to seeing pictures, if revealing features of a scene not visible in seeing the scene face to face modifies subsequent face-to-face experience.

Looking at a picture frequently requires effort, sometimes a great deal of effort, in attention to detail, accurate perception, and adaptable seeing. Thus we are reluctant ever to conclude that we have seen all there is to see in a picture, to 'sum it up' in a single experience. A person who misses the fine details of an image, or who cannot see how it portrays previously unremarked features of reality, or who cannot see things in new way…such a person does not appreciate it fully. In order to meet these demands, viewers must become fine observers. They gain or cement a capacity that is exportable beyond its site of acquisition, either to seeing other pictures or to seeing outside pictures.

The benefits of fine observation are not purely experiential—after all, experience is not quarantined from cognition. A fine observer has visual experiences that closely track the properties of what is perceived and bring her experiences under concepts which make them available to belief formation, knowledge gathering, and reasoning. Pictures have cognitive merit in so far as they bring about revisions to the way we conceptualize visual experience.

Catherine Wilson attributes the cognitive merit of reading literary fiction to 'a modification of a person's concepts, which is in turn capable of altering his thought or conduct, and not primarily to an increased disposition to utter factually correct statements or to display technical prowess' (1983: 495; see also John 1998). This process of conceptual revision requires that a reader first recognize that the conception of a situation presented in a story is superior to her own conception of the situation, and then for this reason adopt the conception so that it governs her behaviour.

Something similar can occur as a result of observing pictures finely. Robert Schwartz argues that, within limits, pictures change our concept of an F by changing what counts for us as an F look-alike. Commenting on Picasso's boast that Gertrude Stein would one day come to look like his portrait of her, Schwartz writes that 'the property "looks like Stein"…requires moulding or shaping. What Picasso does is help make this property the property it is' (1985: 715). Andrew Harrison suggests that Picasso's *Weeping Woman* shifts 'our conception of weeping, outraged female grief, and the outrage of such grief, by the method of representation employed… the picture shows us that that is how we may recognise a particular variety of weeping' (1973: 130–1). Consider how Figure 2 puts pressure on traditional conceptions of looking and the stereotypical gender of the person who looks intensely (see Chapter 5).

In sum, fine observation is one intellectual virtue fostered or reinforced by looking at pictures, and it is a cognitive merit in pictures that boost fine observation. They are training wheels, albeit sometimes very sophisticated training wheels, that enable thinkers to hone their cognitive abilities. By the same token, some pictures have cognitive demerit in so far as they inhibit the exercise or acquisition of fine observation. They deaden attention to detail, solicit inaccurate seeing, weaken adaptive seeing, or instil inferior concepts.

Needless to say, fine observation is not the only intellectual virtue that pictures may foster, reinforce, or undermine. Interpretation, picking up allusions, getting visual puns and jokes: these tasks and others depend upon, and so may foster, several intellectual virtues. We may continue to catalogue the demands that pictures impose upon us and then consider whether they foster intellectual excellence of one kind or another. The enterprise is a worthy one, but undertaking it is not necessary to assess cognitivism.

Aesthetic Ascent

So close is the intuitive tie between knowledge and cognitive value that we take it for granted that any picture of great cognitive merit must add to knowledge. But while some pictures do add to knowledge, the addition does not imply, and is not implied by, any aesthetic evaluation. A narrowly epistemic conception of cognitive value undermines cognitivism. The remedy is to make room for non-epistemic cognitive value—in particular, the value that lies in fostering or undermining intellectual virtues, such as fine observation. It remains to see how an evaluation of a picture for its contribution to fine observation can imply or be implied by an aesthetic evaluation of the picture.

Cognitive—aesthetic

Criticism of pictures is permeated with terms of cognitive praise and reproach. Pictures are judged 'true to life', 'revelatory', 'rich in ideas', 'searching', 'insightful', 'reflective', 'distorted', or 'manipulative', for example. Autonomists say that these evaluations have no aesthetic implications—the evaluation of pictures is a ragbag of unrelated items. The cognitivist counters that some of these evaluations have aesthetic implications—there is unity, if partial, among different kinds of evaluations of pictures. In making a case for this view, we are free to draw upon the conjecture marking the boundaries of aesthetic evaluation.

Two features for which pictures are praised show special promise: being true to life and being revealing. Pictures are true to life when they demand and so foster accurate seeing; they are revealing when they demand and so foster adaptability of seeing. Accuracy and adaptability of seeing are two elements of fine observation.

Suppose that *Migrant Mother* (Fig. 12) is evaluated as true to life, and that the evaluation is an accurate one. Thus it is a cognitive merit in the picture that it is true to life. Maybe this is because the picture communicates a piece of knowledge. That granted, the picture also fosters or reinforces the cognitive virtue of fine observation by boosting accurate seeing. The same goes for a judgement that the photograph is revealing. It may be revealing because it conveys knowledge-in, but it is also revealing in the sense that it fosters and reinforces adaptable seeing.

'*Migrant Mother* is true to life.' This judgement is an aesthetic evaluation if and only if three conditions are satisfied (Chapter 3). First, being true to life must be a merit in *Migrant Mother*. We have already assumed that being true to life is a merit in the picture in the sense that what is true to life fosters or reinforces fine observation. The merit is cognitive. Second, a suitable observer's experience of the picture as true to life must be part of what makes being true to life a merit in the picture. Third, a suitable observer's experience must warrant the judgement.

Only the satisfaction of the second condition is liable to provoke doubt. Moreover, it is the active ingredient distinguishing aesthetic from non-aesthetic evaluations. The question is why we should think that an experience of *Migrant Mother* as true to life is part of what makes being true to life a merit in it. Note that the issue is not whether the picture is true to life only if it is experienced as true to life. Nor is the issue whether being true to life is a merit only if experienced as a merit. It does not matter how those issues are settled. What matters is whether an experience of the picture as true to life is part of what makes that property a merit of the picture.

We know two things. First, *Migrant Mother* is true to life because it boosts accurate seeing, which is part of the virtue of fine observation, and thus its being true to life is a merit in it. The first condition of the internalist conjecture is met. Second, the photograph is seen by a suitable observer as true to life—as making a contribution to a capacity for accurate seeing. Cognitivist and autonomist alike may accept these as facts. They part ways on the question of whether the second fact is part of the first.

Distinguish between two ways in which fostering or reinforcing accurate seeing can be a cognitive merit. If *Migrant Mother* has cognitive merit merely because it is true to life, it has 'ground-level cognitive merit'. This is contrasted with 'step-up cognitive merit'. The photograph has step-up cognitive merit just in case it has cognitive merit because it is true to life and also because part of what makes being true to life a cognitive merit in it is that it is experienced as true to life by a suitable observer.

Notice that an attribution of step-up cognitive merit to a picture meets the second condition of the internalist conjecture and so implies an aesthetic evaluation. Attributions of step-up merits are aesthetic as well as cognitive.

So the issue between cognitivism and autonomism can be reframed using the distinction between ground-level and step-up cognitive merit. For the cognitivist, some pictures have step-up cognitive merit. For the autonomist, all cognitive evaluations of pictures are ground-level: it is never part of what it is for a feature of a picture to be a cognitive (de)merit in it that it is experienced by anyone as having the feature. The (de)meritorious feature can be fully characterized without reference to any experience of the feature.

If this framing of the issues is correct, then the autonomist is saddled with an implausible position. Intellectual virtue admits of degrees. A thinker may be more or less reliable in achieving the cognitive goals that pertain to the exercise of a virtue. She may also act more or less from a motivation associated with a virtue. Pictures with step-up merit especially require and foster high degrees of fine observation.

One reason is that a high degree of intellectual virtue comes with and from an awareness of what activities exercise and strengthen virtue. The point is not specific to intellectual virtue. Part of learning any skill—handling paint, playing the saxophone, or springboard diving, for example—is learning to tell what practices improve the skill and which ones do not. Seeing what improves a skill helps improve it and comes with having improved it. Likewise, seeing what experiences boost fine observation comes with and improves that virtue. A picture experienced as boosting fine observation has a merit not found in a picture which merely boosts fine observation without being seen to do so.

Moreover, if degree of virtue varies with motivation, then pictures have step-up cognitive merit to the extent that they trigger or instil a motivation to fine observation. As already noted, one often gains a virtue through the back door. People look at pictures for enjoyment, to acquire bragging rights, or to learn about the past. Whatever the motivation, the result may be an improvement in fine observation. However, if fine observation has a motivational component, then that motivation is typically what drives high-degree fine observers to exercise the virtue. They try to see pictures finely because they see that pictures are not just opportunities for fine observation but challenges to it. Seeing a picture as a challenge to fine observation provides a reason to exercise or strengthen the virtue. Again, a picture seen as boosting fine observation has a merit not found in a picture which merely boosts fine observation without being seen to do so: its merit lies in its triggering a motivation to see finely.

There is more, then, to step-up merit than ground-level merit. *Migrant Mother* may benefit some people merely by helping them to see more accurately—it has ground-level benefits for them. For those who see it as true to life—as boosting accurate seeing—it has further benefits. When a suitable observer sees it as boosting fine observation and when that experience is part of its cognitive merit, it has step-up cognitive merit and hence aesthetic merit.

If step-up cognitive merits do not reduce to ground-level ones, then findings of step-up cognitive merit imply aesthetic evaluations. Autonomism is consistent with this only if no pictures in fact have step-up merit. Biting that bullet has little to recommend it. Seeing is not lacking in any obvious feature that is present in other kinds of cognition and that would explain the failure of pictures to have step-up cognitive merit. At least, it is up to the autonomist to identify it. In addition, it is not hard to find pictures that are not fully appreciated unless their step-up merit is acknowledged. Chapter 5 presents some cases.

To summarize, step-up cognitive merit is not reducible to ground-level cognitive merit. Some pictures have step-up cognitive merit. But attributions of step-up merit to pictures comply with all three conditions of the internalist conjecture. So some attributions of cognitive merit to pictures imply aesthetic evaluations.

Cognitivist criticism

Sound arguments are not always persuasive. Someone might find that this argument paints an overly intellectualized picture of cognitive evaluation. Do we evaluate pictures as vehicles through which we recognize what experiences boost fine observation? Do we look at pictures and say that they are good because they help us see how to improve our intellectual capabilities? Do we say that they are bad because they make it harder to see how to make those improvements? If we do any of these things, is it with any frequency?

Put this way, the objection seems on target. However, it is important to remember that aesthetic and cognitive evaluation are not well understood, and it is unlikely that our pre-theoretic awareness of what they involve closely tracks what they *do* involve. Moreover, in some criticism, awareness comes close to reality. We say that pictures change our lives and the way we think. When we say this, we usually mean that they *show us how* to change our lives and the way we think. We rarely mean that they merely *cause* a change, like some kind of special medication.

This reply pits intuition against intuition, so it is as unlikely as it is likely to strike a persuasive chord. The argument may still seem to paint an overly intellectualized picture of cognitive evaluation. Three points should soften the objection.

The cognitivist may concede this much: that the argument focuses on an intellectualized tip of a non-intellectualized iceberg. Many straightforwardly ground-level cognitive evaluations of pictures imply aesthetic evaluations of them as true to life. Since implication is transitive, many cognitive evaluations that do not attribute step-up cognitive merit imply aesthetic evaluations. Think of evaluations of *Woman Holding a Balance* as precisely rendered (Fig. 1), of *Woman with Field Glasses* as provocative (Fig. 2), of *A Pair of Shoes* as honest (Fig. 3), of the panel from *Maus* as chilling (Fig. 10), and of *Belshazzar's Feast* as insightful (Fig. 11).

The implications may also run in the opposite direction. Aesthetic evaluations of pictures that imply attributions of accuracy or revelatoriness imply cognitive evaluations. The point can be illustrated using items from Sibley's list of aesthetic terms (which we stipulated in Chapter 3 to be evaluative). The list includes 'unified, balanced, integrated, lifeless, serene, sombre, dynamic, powerful, vivid, delicate, moving, trite, sentimental, tragic' (2001*a*: 1). Part of the reason why the panel from *Maus* (Fig. 10) is true to life is that it is sombre, vivid, and powerful: it could not have these properties unless it were true to life. That is, it could not be vivid, powerful, and moving unless it modulated our vision of its subject; if it left our vision of its subject untouched, it would be lifeless and trite.

Finally, we do not merely see pictures, we see in them the scenes they depict. Seeing-in, especially seeing-in pictures that are interesting to see things in, draws attention to the activity of seeing, its quality and its contribution to cognition. We should expect that pictures that have high aesthetic merit specifically because they are vehicles for seeing-in tend also to have high cognitive merit.

Fine seeing-in

Some cognitive evaluations of pictures imply aesthetic evaluations, but it does not follow that some cognitive evaluations of pictures as vehicles for seeing-in imply aesthetic evaluations of them as vehicles for seeing-in. A defence of cognitivism must attend to this wrinkle. Evaluations of pictures as true to life are the easy case. Instead, consider evaluations of pictures as revealing in the sense that they demand, and so foster, adaptability of seeing.

Chapter 1 made a case for pluralism about seeing-in. Seeing-in comes in several forms, each characterized by its relationship with design seeing (Table 1). Moreover, the different forms of seeing-in are manifest inter- and intra-pictorially.

In some pictures seeing-in doubles with design seeing, so that one sees the design as undergirding the depicted scene. Seeing-in and design seeing meld into one experience. In other pictures, seeing-in divides from design seeing, so that it is necessary to switch between seeing scene and design. When seeing-in divides from surface seeing, the result is *trompe-l'œil*. Only in *trompe-l'œil* is seeing in the picture phenomenally indistinguishable from seeing the depicted scene face to face. In all other cases, the scene may be depicted as looking as it does not look face to face.

Few pictures fall entirely within one of these classes, though. Most pictures *trompe l'œil* when it comes to some properties, double seeing-in with design seeing when it comes to other properties, and divide seeing-in from design seeing when it comes to a third set of properties. They are mixed bags.

Pictures are eye-openers. They reveal aspects of the world that we would not have seen otherwise, and this benefits us. Without doubt some pictures are revelatory in the sense that they transmit novel pieces of knowledge. These pictures have cognitive merit because knowledge is a cognitive good. At the same time, some pictures are revelatory in the sense that they enhance our capability to see what would otherwise remain invisible. They foster and reinforce adaptable seeing. Adaptable seeing is a component of fine observation, which is a virtue because those who possess it reliably attain their cognitive goals. It is therefore a cognitive merit in a picture if it is revealing in this sense, and a cognitive demerit in it if it undermines adaptability of seeing.

An evaluation of a picture as revelatory is an evaluation of it as a vehicle for seeing-in if the evaluation is explained by appeal to what is seen in the picture by a suitable observer. Suppose that a suitable observer sees Daumier's drawing *Fatherly Discipline* (Fig. 8) as revelatory in the virtue-theoretic sense. Her evaluation is an evaluation of the picture as a picture if it is explained by her seeing something in the picture and by how her experience of seeing-in relates to experiences of the picture's surface.

The title-figure in Daumier's drawing expresses a mixture of frustration, anger, and helplessness—and these expressions are seen in the picture (Chapter 2). However, the father figure does not look at all like a frustrated, angry, and helpless person would look when seen face to face. The design of the father's face is seen alongside the face itself, and that design contributes to the figure's expression. For example, the emphatic X-shaped lines around his eyes express a concentration that is countermanded by the chaotic lines used to render the rest of his face and to express helpless loss of control. A mix of emotions is made visible in a way that cannot be achieved in ordinary visual experience.

Not every picture that shows something otherwise invisible is revealing; a revealing picture boosts adaptability of seeing. This result can be achieved in two ways. First, by revealing features of a scene not visible in seeing the scene face to face, a picture may modify subsequent face-to-face experiences of the scene—or ones like it in relevant respects. Exposure to *Fatherly Discipline* may tweak its viewer's capacity to see what is expressed by angrily exasperated parents. Second, a picture's revealing features of a scene not visible in seeing it face to face may leverage conceptual revision. Serious attention given to Daumier's drawing may revise the way we think about the stresses of parenting.

Getting right the cognitive value of pictures as vehicles for seeing-in means having the right conception of cognitive value. While we do get knowledge from seeing things in pictures, this has little to do with their aesthetic merit. No matter its aesthetic merit, it is unlikely that we come to *know* anything by seeing figures' expressions in *Fatherly Discipline*—Daumier is not an expert in psychology. However, his drawing may well contribute to or subvert the intellectual virtue of fine observation in a way that has precisely to do with its aesthetic value as a vehicle for seeing-in.

Interactionism is true if cognitivism is true. Cognitivism has the best chance of being true if the cognitive value of some pictures lies in their capacity to cement or subvert intellectual virtue. Part of that capacity, when the intellectual virtue in question is fine observation, is the capacity to prompt experiences of seeing-in. Therefore, some cognitive evaluations of pictures as vehicles for seeing-in imply or are implied by some aesthetic evaluations of pictures as vehicles for seeing-in. Die-hard autonomists who reject this conclusion are not left empty-handed, though. They may agree with the cognitivist that pictures can have value not only as instruments for knowing-in but also as aids to fine seeing-in.

5   MORAL VISION

Man is a creature who makes pictures of himself
and then comes to resemble the pictures.

Iris Murdoch

We sometimes evaluate pictures by moral criteria. De Kooning's
Woman series has been castigated as coarsely misogynistic. Arthur
Danto commends the photographs in Robert Mapplethorpe's
X Portfolio as intimate and respectful (Danto 1996). It is hard to
conceive of a sound discussion of *Guernica* with nothing to say about
the humanistic principles it embodies, just as it is hard to overlook
the crass eroticization of a great human evil in Gérôme's *Slave Market*.
According to moralism, some moral evaluations of pictures imply
or are implied by aesthetic evaluations of them. Moral criticisms of
De Kooning's women and Gérôme's *Slave Market* may imply aesthetic
criticisms. The moral appreciation of X Portfolio and *Guernica* may
imply aesthetic praise. Moral and aesthetic evaluation interact.

Content and Evaluation

Moralists must shoulder a burden that does not encumber cognit-
ivists. Nobody since Plato has denied that some pictures have
cognitive merit, but some think that pictures never have significant
moral merit. Moreover, nobody—not even Plato—seriously suggests
that pictures are not legitimate targets of cognitive evaluation, so one
might wonder whether it makes any sense to subject them to moral
evaluation.

In some ways, pictures are uncontroversially targets of moral
evaluation. After all, they are artefacts whose making and display

have consequences for human life. A well-known recent example from sculpture is the controversy over the installation of Richard Serra's *Tilted Arc* in the New York Federal Plaza. Many users of the plaza complained that, whatever its aesthetic virtues, Serra's piece made the place hostile and uninhabitable, and this was taken by all but its most fanatic defenders as a legitimate though perhaps inconclusive reason to remove it (Weyergraf-Serra and Buskirk 1988). In just the same way, the beneficial or injurious consequences of making a picture or of putting it on display give us good reasons to praise or blame it from a moral point of view. To evaluate a work in this way is to evaluate it as an artefact like any other artefact, to apply to it the standards of moral evaluation proper to artefacts of any kind.

The concession does not end matters, though. We may still wonder whether pictures are legitimate targets of moral evaluation specifically as vehicles for seeing-in.

Standard lists of the targets of moral evaluation include persons, their motivations, and their actions. In addition, utterances and beliefs are sometimes targets of moral evaluation as regards their contents, provided that the contents are moral ones. Some moral beliefs and expressions are said to be admirable, while others are said to be reprehensible. The proposition that we should redistribute to the needy as much of our individual wealth as is consistent with not reducing the wealth of all is morally admirable. The proposition that rape is a permissible instrument of war is morally disgusting. By contrast, non-moral propositions (e.g. 'The health benefits of vitamins are exaggerated') are not normally subject to moral evaluation (though moral propositions may appear in non-moral disguise, as in 'The Holocaust is a myth').

One might object that it is an illusion that moral propositions are proper targets of moral evaluation. According to this objection, only the *acts* of believing or asserting moral propositions are legitimate targets of moral evaluation, though we tend to confuse evaluations of those acts with evaluations of the contents believed or asserted. This will not do, however. You may approve, from a moral point of view, the trumpeting of unpopular moral stances by Ralph Nader or Rush Limbaugh (choose one) while condemning as immoral the stances trumpeted (choose the other). Moral beliefs and assertions are subject to moral scrutiny for their contents, independently of the acts of believing or asserting them.

How are pictures to be evaluated for their moral contents?

One answer is that they are evaluated for the beneficial or injurious consequences that flow from their depicting what they do. An image that inspires just rebellion by depicting an outrage may be commended for its content; one that ignites racial hostilities by depicting racial slanders may be condemned for its content. Sceptics retort that the effects of picture viewing on people's actions, beliefs, and attitudes cannot be measured well enough to justify any evaluation. To make matters worse, there is no systematic connection between prima-facie moral evaluations of pictures for their contents and the consequences of their being made or put on display. A picture that depicts racial slanders may, by confronting us with the extent of human malice, better prepare us to contend with it.

Consider another answer. Sometimes, to criticize a representation as morally repugnant is to say that it is cognitively flawed as regards its moral content, and to praise it as morally admirable is to say that it is cognitively sound as regards its moral content. For example, it may be flawed because its moral content is false, or sound because its moral content is true. The moral evaluation of pictures is a species of cognitive evaluation. An account of it requires a moral epistemology as well as a conception of the contents of pictures.

If the proposal is that moral evaluations of representations are cognitive evaluations of moral contents, then why regard them as moral evaluations at all? Why not think that we simply confuse cognitive evaluations of representations as regards their moral contents with moral evaluations? Why not be purists and confine the objects of moral evaluation to persons, motivations, and actions?

Settling this matter would carry us far afield, into unexplored regions of moral theory and epistemology. Prudence dictates submitting to common usage: some moral evaluations are cognitive evaluations of representations as regards their moral contents. Sceptics about the thesis that pictures are legitimate targets of moral evaluation may appeal the move on grounds that it begs the question. We should deny the appeal. It is sufficient to answer sceptics about the moral evaluation of pictures specifically as vehicles for seeing-in.

The same reasoning justifies shrugging off blanket rejections of moral evaluation as either incoherent or as thinly disguised political ideology. Lucy Lippard observes that morality is 'generally avoided in high-art "discourse", where the word "moral" is usually considered either laughable, rhetorical and/or the property of the right' (1992: 203). Blanket scepticism about moral evaluation does not fully explain scepticism targeted specifically at the moral evaluation of pictures. The latter is wont to persist despite the demise of the former.

Mimesis and Moral Vision

The moralist must trace and eradicate scepticism that springs from our conception of picturing itself. The sceptic who trades on the fact that pictures are mimetic need not take issue with those who argue that stories can have quite significant moral content (Novitz 1987; Booth 1988; Nussbaum 1990; Stephen Davies 1997; Levinson 1998; Carroll 2000; Bermudez and Gardner 2003). On the contrary, this body of work provides the sceptic with a powerful strategy: to argue that since stories have moral content in virtue of features that pictures lack, the reason why stories have moral content indicates why pictures lack it. The strategy is to show that pictures are not apt targets of evaluation as regards their moral contents because they have no moral contents.

Narrative morality

Here is an argument that implements this strategy: stories are morally informative because moral action is describable only by narratives (or theories), but pictures are not narrative (or theoretic) representations, so pictures cannot have serious moral content.

The first premiss, that moral content can be conveyed only by means of narrative (or theory), is a thesis of moral epistemology. Some argue more strongly that only stories, and not moral philosophy, can access important regions of morality. As Martha Nussbaum writes, 'certain truths about human life can only be fittingly and accurately stated in the language and forms of the narrative artist' (1990: 5). The sceptic is not committed to this stronger claim. It is enough for her to show that, alongside moral philosophy, only narrative representation can convey moral truths.

Why is narrative a particularly suitable tool for making moral discoveries? The answer has to do both with the nature of narrative and with a conception of the nature of morality, for narratives exploit the fact that moral agency is temporal. This fact is given expression in the following definition of narrative which, though rough, is ready enough for present purposes. A narrative is a representation of events (1) as ordered in time, (2) as actions, and (3) as seen from the point of view of agents.

Beginning with (2), an action is a behaviour carried out by a person for a reason—that is, when her desires, feelings, preferences, beliefs, commitments, intentions, or goals play a role in generating or causing her behaviour. What a narrative does is to make events intelligible by linking them in the mental lives of rational agents. Since moral acts are one kind of act, narratives may represent moral acts.

Granted, psychological descriptions and even moral philosophy can also represent events as moral acts and agents as moved by or sensitive to moral considerations. Clause (3) of the definition adds that narratives represent the considerations that move agents as seen from the point of view of agents—that is, from the points of view of characters in a story, the story's narrator, its implied author, or sometimes even its implied reader. This is what sets story telling apart from scientific and philosophical accounts of human behaviour, which represent human affairs from an impersonal, third-person perspective.

The conjunction of (2) and (3) indicates why one might think that stories have serious moral content. In order to grasp a story that shows how actions and events appear from an agent's point of view, given her moral sensitivities, concerns, and commitments, we must imaginatively adopt her point of view (Kieran 1996; Currie 1997, 1998). When this point of view is quite different from that of actual readers, a story may spotlight features of situations of which its readers might otherwise have remained unaware. Taking the point of view prescribed by a story can bring otherwise obscure features of a situation into sight.

The second premiss of the sceptic's argument is that pictures are not narratives, and this also seems right. True, some pictures are parts of narratives—comic books and their precursors, such as Spiegelman's *Maus* and Hogarth's *Rake's Progress*, tell stories as much by means of graphic representation as by means of text. The obvious reply is that comic books and the like tell stories only by means of a sequence of images. The sceptic may happily concede that sequences of images such as *Maus* have moral content because they represent events unfolding in time. Sequential pictures that have moral content have it only in so far as they are like stories, and so, the sceptic goes on to maintain, single images cannot narrate action and therefore lack moral content.

The sceptic's concession invites a question. Exactly what is it about single pictures that precludes their representing narratives? At this point the argument appeals to the mimetic character of pictures. Images do not have narrative content, for, unlike works in other media, they show how things look.

Susan Sontag gave the argument its classic statement. 'Photography', she writes,

implies that we know about the world if we accept it as the camera records it. But this is the opposite of understanding which starts from not accepting the world as it looks. … In contrast to the amorous relation, which is based on how something looks, understanding is based on how it functions. And functioning takes place in time, and must be explained in time. … The limit of photographic knowledge of the world is that, while it can goad conscience, it can, finally, never be ethical or political knowledge. (1979: 23)

Sontag's worry generalizes from photographs to paintings, drawings, and prints. While a photograph is, according to Sontag, an instantaneous 'registering of an emanation (light waves reflected by objects)', paintings and drawings are the products of a lengthy creative process (1979: 154). The trouble with this way of distinguishing photographic from hand-made images is that it confuses the instantaneity of the photo-making process with the depiction of instantaneity. It does not follow from the fact that an image is created in a moment of time that it cannot represent events as extended in time. A photograph of a skydiver shows her as falling by registering one moment of the fall—it does not represent her as suspended, frozen in mid-air! Conversely, many a painting, made painstakingly over several weeks, captures a fleeting moment.

The true source of Sontag's worry is not that photographs depict instants, but that they merely convey how things look. The active ingredient in her argument is not the distinction between mechanically made and hand-made pictures, but rather the distinction between the kind of understanding that is based on 'how something looks' and the kind of understanding that is based on 'how it functions'—between mimesis and narrative.

Sontag's argument boasts a distinguished ancestry and was familiar to an earlier age primarily through Lessing (1962; see Savile 1986: 34–6). Since pictures merely show us the appearance of things, they cannot narrate action; and since only narrative (or theoretical) works can convey moral content, they lack moral content.

Moral space

One reply to the sceptic's argument concedes that only narrative (or theoretical) works may have moral content but argues that pictures can narrate action. The idea is that pictures represent space, which is a medium in which action takes place.

The historian William Ivins pointed out that the great accomplishment of the early Renaissance, the invention of systematic perspective, was ancillary to a need to construct an arena for the representation of action. As Ivins puts it, 'across the centuries the religious subject matter of art gradually becomes dramatic. This drama was full of action. Action implies relationships between human figures located in the same visual spaces' (1962: 62). Thus Alberti, whose project was the project of the Renaissance, insisted that 'the greatest work of the painter is *istoria*'—the representation of action (1966: 70).

The depiction of space in perspective makes this possible in two ways. A picture may represent action by representing movement through space, or, since human action is directed at objects and people, it may represent action by showing where agents are located in relation to other objects or people. A picture of Charon with an oar and one of his unfortunate passengers with her arm raised represents two actions—of attack and defence—because it represents the oar as being swung at the woman and her arm being raised to parry the blow. It is difficult not to think this obvious, but for Alberti the development of techniques allowing for the representation of objects moving in relation to each other was an enormous advance.

Incidentally, Alberti does not contradict Lessing's doctrine that 'the artist can never use more of ever-changing reality than one single moment of time' (1962: sect. 3). He sees that movement need not be represented by movement and that a person's action can be represented as movement by locating it in a context of objects and other persons.

Wittgenstein said that 'the human body is the best picture of the human soul' (1953: 178). He is thinking not only of movements but of expressive gestures and postures. Since emotions are not mere reactions to happenings, but also motivate actions, expression is a route to understanding events as actions. Pictures that depict gestures and facial expressions reveal the mental states of depicted figures and thereby represent their actions as actions—the raising

of an arm is made intelligible as action by the expression of fear
with which it is done (Tilghman 1996). Leonardo added expression
to bodily movement as a way to depict *istoria*: since 'the most
important in painting are the movements originating from the
mental state of living creatures, the movements, that is, appropriate
to the state of... desire, contempt, anger or pity', the artist should
carefully observe 'those who talk together with gesticulating hands,
and get near to listen to what makes them make that particular
gesture' (quoted in Gombrich 1982*a*: 68).

The sceptic argues that a non-theoretic representation has
serious moral content only if it represents action as action, that
pictures cannot narrate action, therefore that pictures can have no
serious moral content. However, if depicted space is one in which
action and the expression of action-guiding emotion can be represented, then it is an arena in which action can be represented as
action. The dramatic spaces depicted by pictures are arenas for
moral dramas which convey serious moral messages.

This response to the sceptic inspires another, for pictures create
spaces that they do not depict. Pictures are not only perceptual
representations in which we see things, they are also physical objects
in our environment. Susan Feagin notes that, as physical objects, pictures 'move out of the realm of "pure" perception and into the
realm of action', thereby relating 'physically to our whole body,
not just to our eyes' (1995: 21). An altar-piece transforms the space
around it by making certain devotions and rituals appropriate.
Seventeenth-century Dutch *vanitas* paintings transform bourgeois
domestic spaces by inviting their inhabitants to reflect on the
impermanence of worldly possessions. By transforming the space
we occupy, pictures can be 'provocations to act in various ways'
(Feagin 1995: 25).

Provocations to act may be moral provocations. Pictures may
bear moral content by placing their viewers in imaginative spaces
in which they are to consider themselves as agents. Consider, for
example, the famous photograph of a Vietnamese child running
naked and terrified down a highway from an aerial attack, towards

an implied viewer. The image does not merely evoke strong emotions or show what it is like to be under attack. It transforms the space in which it is displayed, prompting its viewers to think about how they ought to respond or will respond.

Beyond mimesis

Unfortunately, both responses arm the sceptic with a reply. If the content of pictures is mimetic, then any interest we have in looking at them is in point of fact an interest in the dramatic scenes they represent and not in their depiction of those scenes.

After all, perspective and expression are needed precisely as instruments to accurately render reality. So perhaps what moves us as we look at the *Raft of the Medusa* is only its subject, the sufferings inflicted upon sailors by a negligent French Navy. Likewise, the capacity of pictures to put us in a space where we may contemplate opportunities for action derives from their capacity to imitate and thereby project spaces. The photograph of the Vietnamese girl relies for its effect on its strong central perspective, for this is what makes the depicted scene part of the space occupied by its viewers, prompting them to imagine how they might and should act. If this is so, then it is not the picture itself which so outrages us but the absent scene it re-creates. The image is simply a portal that puts us in its subject's space. Indeed, pictures are more effective at prompting moral reflection the more closely they approach an ideal of illusionism and the less they figure as objects of attention in their own right.

This reasoning obviously depends on the conception of pictorial mimesis that generates the puzzle of mimesis. To see this, consider why the deflationary reply should not be interpreted as applying to stories as much as to pictures. A story uses language to describe scenes, characters, and actions, but our sceptic will not claim that in reading literature our attention is directed at the scenes, characters, and actions described, rather than at the description of them.

She must hold instead that it is in the nature of depiction that seeing a depicted scene totally displaces seeing the depiction of the scene. It is precisely this view of pictures that generates the puzzle of mimesis.

In order to respond to scepticism about the moral content of pictures, we must explain how a more capacious conception of mimetic content accommodates moral content. Ideally, we should show that pictures may have serious moral content without depicting the actions of agents—just because they sustain seeing-in.

A picture of the human soul

Pictures may have non-narrative moral content, specifically because they are vehicles for seeing-in.

Consider illustrations of Dante's *Inferno*. The *Commedia* has appeared in a great many illustrated editions, and these illustrations recap the history of pictures in the West: anything that can be done with pictures has probably been attempted in some illustration of the *Inferno* (see Nassar 1994). Moreover, many artists remark upon the vividness and force of Dante's visual descriptions. Tom Phillips writes that 'Dante's powers of physical visualization (in which he parallels his friend Giotto in his new bodying forth of the world's reality) are unprecedented in literature' (Dante 1985*a*: 296). These visual descriptions are a case of making a virtue of necessity, for although the *Inferno* narrates the Pilgrim's journey through hell and the resulting maturation of his character, when the poem turns to the denizens of hell, narrative is no longer possible. The condemned were once moral agents who shaped their lives through their actions, but they are supposed in the afterlife to have lost their freedom and are no longer capable of action. We get to know them only through their histories and through Dante's physical descriptions.

Many illustrations of the *Inferno* have narrative moral content. An example is an eighteenth-century Venetian engraving (Fig. 13) which depicts the Pilgrim's encounter with the punishment of the

Fig. 13. Workshop of Antonio Zatta, *Inferno* XXIV, 1757–8.

thieves. In the engraving, Virgil's gesture signifies his role as teacher, and the Pilgrim's posture betrays the emotional impact on him of what he is learning. The landscape in which the thieves are placed—a deep, confining pit—conveys a sense of the inescapability of their punishment. The punishment itself is terrible, and the suffering it brings can be read on the face of the figure to the left. Through gesture, facial expression, and the placement of figures in space, this picture portrays both an episode of the principal narrative of the *Inferno*—the Pilgrim's education—and a scene of infernal punishment.

While images such as this bring to life the scenes before the narrator's eyes and chill the reader's blood, they usually fail to convey the moral ideas at the heart of the poem. The *Inferno* is not a horror show or a parade of phantoms. Robin Kirkpatrick describes the *Commedia* as a 'portrait of all of human activity, a great mechanism for the precise definition of terms such as "virtue", "knowledge", and "love" ' (1987: 72). To this end, the landscape of hell is laid out as a map of human vice, in each region of which the damned are punished in a specific way that not only fits but also reveals their vicious character. The engraving is horrific perhaps, but it is no emblem of the nature of theft.

Commentators describe the punishments of Dante's hell as *contrapasso*. The word appears only once in the poem, uttered by the decapitated schismatic troubadour Bertran de Born, who, having caused a father and son to rebel against each other, admits:

> Because I parted their union, I carry my brain
> Parted from this, its pitiful stem: Mark well
> This retribution [*contrapasso*] that you see is mine
>
> (Dante 1994: XXVIII. 139–42)

This translation of *contrapasso* as 'retribution' is not wholly inaccurate. Dante derives the term from the Latin word coined to translate Aristotle's *antipeponthos*—'the state of suffering something in return'. This appears to be how Bertran views his punishment. But this view of *contrapasso* leaves mysterious why each punishment is so exquisitely and grotesquely fitted to each vice, as the case of Bertran himself illustrates.

Dante's conception of *contrapasso* must be grasped in the context of his ethics and metaphysics. Dante thinks of virtues and vices as states of character that one acquires as a consequence of one's actions and that dispose one to do virtuous or vicious deeds (Minio-Paluello 1980). Moreover, these states of character are cognitive states, steady dispositions to desire to act in certain ways, as circumstances warrant. Dante's philosophy of mind is equally indebted to Aristotle: cognitive states are states of the soul, the *anima humana*, which structures and animates a material frame (Boyd 1993: 160). So, if one's character is a state of one's *anima*, and if the *anima* is the *forma* of one's body, then one's body should reveal one's moral character. This thinking accounts for Dante's interest in the gestures, facial expressions, and other 'outward looks that bear witness to the heart' (Dante 1985*b*: XXVIII. 44–5).

The dead, however, have lost their bodies, and are nothing but *ombre* or 'shades'. In *Purgatory* XXV, the Pilgrim encounters the emaciated bodies of gluttons and wonders how a shade, which has no need of food, can grow so lean. The answer reveals Dante's metaphysics of the afterlife. Upon death, the part of the *anima humana* that is responsible for cognitive functions survives, but since it must give form to a body, it irradiates the surrounding atmosphere 'to reshape what the body had before' (Dante 1985*b*: XXV. 90). If moral character is a steady disposition to desire to act in certain ways in appropriate conditions, if this disposition is a state of the *anima*, and if the *anima* gives shape to the *ombra*, then it follows that the *ombra* 'takes on the form of our desire' and visibly manifests our moral character (Dante 1985*b*: XXV. 106). In Dante's scheme, there is an internal connection between vice and punishment. The agonies expressed through the bodies of the damned externalize and fulfil their vicious characters. Their *contrapasso* consists in the uninhibited and hence ironic physical embodiment of their own desires. A description of the punishment of each vice is a lesson on the nature of that vice (see Stump 1986).

Needless to say, Dante's metaphysics is fantastical. We do best simply to treat the doctrine of *contrapasso* as a fiction. Nevertheless, if it is a literary device, it may be one by means of which we may learn something about human character. The same may be said for its pictorial analogue.

The idea of *contrapasso* serves as a device that some illustrators have successfully used to convey, in a distinctively pictorial form, some of Dante's moral ideas. If the 'punishments' of the damned reveal the states of their *anima* as they are inscribed upon their bodies, then we may allow the surface of an image to stand for the space a person's *anima* occupies, on to which it stamps its character. A portrait of a damned soul is then a space transformed so as to reveal the character of its subject. Such a portrait need not accurately render its subject's outward appearance or actions.

Take as a first example Tom Phillips's print for Canto xxviii (Fig. 14). In keeping with the doctrine of *contrapasso*, Dante has the schismatics cut limb from limb—the canto is the bloodiest in the *Inferno*. What attracts most illustrators is the opportunity to depict such grisly sights,

> As the man I saw split open from his chin
> Down to the farting-place, and from the splayed
> Trunk the spilled entrails dangled between his thighs
> I saw his organs, and the sack that makes the bread
> We swallow turn to shit

> (Dante 1994: xxviii. 23–7)

Literal depictions, such as Gustave Doré's (Fig. 15), emphasize the gruesome, but distract us from the point of the canto or, at best, encourage a lazy grasp of the *contrapasso*, as 'those who cause rifts among people shall be split themselves'.

Phillips attempts to see through the gore. His print began as a paper chain, of the kind that children make, that he used as a stencil to print a lattice of human figures. We see that each individual is connected to all others, and that this 'community' is nothing but the network of its individual members. Here and there the lattice is torn, in an obvious representation of schism. But what is interesting

Fig. 14. Tom Phillips, frontispiece for *Inferno* xxviii, 1985. © DACS/SODART 2004.

is that the tears in the 'social fabric' are always, and can only be, located within individuals. The schismatics are not mutilated *because* they rend the fabric of society; they are mutilated because to rend the fabric of society just is to rend themselves. Phillips's picture expresses the idea visually.

Fig. 15. Gustave Doré, *Inferno* XXVIII, 1861.

The idea connects to contemporary debates in ethics. Many will be puzzled or offended by Dante's treatment of schism. Consider substituting 'discord' or 'dissent' for the almost archaic 'schism': we no longer regard disagreement as a serious moral infraction. Be that as it may, some have argued that familiar liberal arguments for tolerating and even encouraging dissent depend on an 'atomistic' conception of the self. Communitarian critics of this conception argue that the self is formed and can maintain its identity only in the context of a community sharing a unity of value and belief. Thus, whatever a communitarian might say about the circumstances under which discord or dissent ought to be tolerated or promoted, she will in some cases conceptualize it not only as dividing a community but as *thereby* fracturing the selves who make up the community. Phillips's illustration depicts this thought simply and elegantly.

Canto xxv contains what must be two of the most astonishing scenes of bodily transformation in the *Inferno*. In one scene, a serpent entwines itself around a thief: 'they clung and made a bond/And mixed their colors' until they became 'neither two nor one' and 'both were lost' (Dante 1994: xxv. 61–2, 69, 72). In the second, a serpent transfixes a thief with its gaze, and the two exchange forms: the one grows hair, the other a forked tongue and eyes on its temples; the one's hind legs twist together to form a penis while from the other's two feet emerge. The narrator boasts that he has outdone Ovid's telling of Cadmus's metamorphosis into a snake:

> He never transformed two individual
> Front-to-front *natures* so both *forms* as they met
> Were ready to exchange their *substance*

> (Dante 1994: xxv. 100–2)

Nicole Pinsky comments that 'these thieves who ignored the boundary of *thine* and *mine* in life now merge as shades, their shells of personal identity made horribly permeable' (Dante 1994: 412). For Dante, each being is by nature an 'informed' substance, but thieves grasp at substance that is not theirs, dispossessing themselves of their own substance and alienating themselves from their own nature.

In the usual manner of illustrating these scenes, a man is shown struggling to free himself from the embrace of an enormous serpent, and if these illustrations succeed at all and do not merely look silly, it is only because they are sufficiently gruesome. Few manage to convey the sense of the *contrapasso*. Rico Lebrun does not attempt a literal portrayal, but instead equates the picture surface with the thief's body, and works transformations upon it equivalent to those the thieves undergo (Fig. 16). What first strikes the viewer is that there is no clear boundary in Lebrun's image between figure and ground.

Fig. 16. Rico Lebrun, *Metamorphosis of Figure into Snake* (*Inferno* xxv), 1961, pen and ink on paper, 40″ × 27¾″. Courtesy of the Estate of Rico Lebrun and Koplin Del Rio Gallery, West Hollywood, Calif.

Lebrun has remarked that in drawings, 'line functions as sandbags do in a flood, according to the pressure of emergency' (1968: 26). In this drawing, the sandbags have reached the point of saturation and are almost overwhelmed. This is not to say that the figure is effaced: we do see an organic mass, but one whose limits and parts shift and shuffle. As a result, the picture compels us to switch back and forth between seeing the masses of light and dark ink on its surface and striving to see an inchoate anatomy. It is as if the material from which the image is made is in possession of competing forms.

Pictures may bear moral content by narrating actions or by depicting persons as having moral qualities. Recognizing that something is depicted as having some moral quality requires exercising and sometimes also acquiring or realigning moral concepts. These moral concepts have a special property: they are applied on the basis of seeing, including seeing in a picture, so they are at once pictorial and moral concepts. We may come to think of dissent or theft differently as a result of seeing bodies in torn cut-out dolls or seeing multiple bodies in masses of ink. We may also resist the conceptual innovations a picture proposes, finding them abhorrent, as distorting moral vision.

Moralism

Moralism is the thesis that some aesthetic evaluations of pictures imply, or are implied by, evaluations of pictures as regards their moral contents. The sceptic rejects moralism because she holds that no pictures have serious moral contents. Autonomists reject moralism for another reason. While granting that pictures may have serious moral content, they deny that evaluations of pictures for their moral content stand in any logical connection to aesthetic evaluations. The relative plausibility of moralism and autonomism depends on how each understands the evaluation of pictures for their moral contents.

There is little hope for moralism if we assume that pictures are to be evaluated for their contribution to moral knowledge. The reasons are familiar. The moral truths to which pictures are apt to give voice are trivial or familiar (Stolnitz 1992). It is hardly news that we ought to help the poor. Setting this aside, the use of a picture to assert a moral truth rarely warrants believing it. When warrant is present, it does not imply, nor is it implied by, findings of aesthetic merit.

Moral knowledge is a cognitive good, but so is anything that makes one an effective moral thinker. An effective moral thinker is not simply a person with a lot of moral knowledge; she possesses 'moral sensibility'—a suite of intellectual resources that makes her reliable in discriminating morally relevant features of situations and gaining moral knowledge. Part of moral sensibility is a repertoire of moral concepts. Given different repertoires of moral concepts, people acquire different moral knowledge and discriminate morally relevant features of situations with varying degrees of accuracy and grain. Moral sensibilities are apt targets for evaluation.

We need not list every resource that goes into moral sensibility or even assume that it is invariable from person to person. It is enough to show that pictures contribute to moral sensibility as vehicles for seeing-in.

The case has already been made if moral sensibility includes possession of a repertoire of moral concepts. Illustrations of the *Inferno*, for instance, may be evaluated for the impact of their mimetic contents on their viewers' moral concepts. The experiences of seeing-in that these pictures require is morally inflected: they depict persons and scenes as having visible properties, and seeing the properties depicted cannot be separated from exercising moral concepts. Evaluations of these illustrations for their impact of moral conceptual repertoires and hence moral sensibility are moral-cognitive evaluations (see also Wilson 1983; John 1998; Carroll 1998: 325–30).

So far, so good, but do evaluations of pictures for their impact on moral sensibility imply aesthetic evaluations? They do, if the boost that a picture applies to moral sensibility is a step-up moral merit in the picture (see Chapter 4). That is, they do if part of the boost to moral sensibility comes from a suitable observer's experience of the boost as a merit. The question we are left with is whether it is part of developing a mature, sophisticated, reliable moral sensibility that one display an awareness of what activities—what kinds of thinking and perceiving—strengthen the sensibility. Attributions of step-up merits, we have seen, are aesthetic evaluations.

Just Looking

The truth of moralism does not ensure it a role in shaping the practice of picture criticism. Moreover, arguments for it are unlikely to catch hold of practising critics unless they address the concerns that make autonomism so appealing. For example, some feminist theorists have mounted the most sustained and systematic attack on depiction since the iconoclasts, arguing that pictures require or engender a 'male gaze' that oppresses women. Current theories of the male gaze imply a wholesale rejection of aesthetic evaluation that is at odds with moralism. Is it possible to develop a moralist criticism of the male gaze?

The male gaze

Feminists have long maintained that the contents of many pictures are sexist, and thus morally reprehensible. The theory of the male gaze promises to explain the psychological origins and effects of these images, and thus to plumb the depth of their moral malignancy.

Debate among feminists about the psychological origins of the male gaze and its oppressive powers should not obscure the feminist consensus about its basic mechanism. John Berger supplies the classic formulation in speaking of the genre of the nude, in which 'men act and women appear. Men look at women. Women watch themselves being looked at. This determines not only most relations between men and women but also the relation of women to themselves… she turns herself into an object—and most particularly an object of vision: a sight' (1972: 47). The male gaze is a way of looking at women merely as things to be looked at.

Although the male gaze is not necessarily pictorial, since it carries over to looking at women in the flesh, it is certainly reflected in and perhaps promoted by certain ways of depicting women. Laura Mulvey points out three ways in which pictures enlist the male gaze (Mulvey 1989; see Devereaux 1995). First, the posing of female figures, the articulation and selection of space around them, the positioning of their imagined viewers, and even the handling of paint may promote the thought that depicted women are merely things to be looked at. Second, male figures who are depicted as looking at female figures model the gendered division of labour between the gazer and the objects of his gaze. Work on the male gaze following the 'image studies' paradigm explores the dynamics of the male gaze as it is deployed in each of these first two ways. It emphasizes how particular pictures display the female body and represent male figures as models of men looking at women.

A third way in which pictures are thought to enlist the male gaze applies to all pictures: it is held that looking at pictures replicates looking at women. As W. J. T. Mitchell puts it, 'paintings, like women, are ideally silent, beautiful creatures, designed for the gratification of the eye, in contrast to the sublime eloquence proper to the manly art of poetry. Paintings are confined to the narrow sphere of external display of their bodies and of the space which they ornament' (1986: 110). Griselda Pollock (1988) puts the point by saying that the picture itself is looked at as a woman, in light of the equations woman = picture and picture-viewer = male.

In her influential essay on the male gaze in film, Mulvey (1989) rejected the image studies paradigm and laid the framework for a new paradigm—call it the 'orthodox account' of the male gaze. The orthodox account foregrounds the third way in which pictures recruit the male gaze and explores how the medium of depiction itself, as opposed to the contents of individual images, reflects ideology. Thus one element of the orthodox account is the proposition that all images mediate the male gaze, and therefore play a special role in the oppression of women.

An additional element of the orthodox account explains why the gaze is necessarily male by appeal to psychoanalysis. The thought is that pictures deliver visual pleasure which is gendered because it issues from the same subconscious erotic events that give rise to gender, so pictures deliver pleasures that are aligned according to gender and have an erotic tint.

Proponents of this account disagree about which psychological events and anxieties precipitate the formation of a gender identity and thereby determine the form of visual pleasures. According to Mulvey, the male gaze subserves either voyeuristic pleasure that re-enacts and so somehow allays castration anxiety or else fetishistic pleasure that denies the anxiety altogether. The details of Mulvey's account have come in for considerable criticism. They do not explain the pleasure women derive from being the objects of the male gaze (Kaplan 1983); nor do they accommodate contextual factors, such as race, class, or history. Finally, it is doubtful that all viewing pleasures are rewards for allaying deep psychological anxieties (Carroll 1995). These controversies about the psychological mechanisms that underlie the male gaze need not detain us, for the only features of the orthodox account that are pertinent here are uncontested among its proponents.

In sum, the orthodox account of the male gaze comprises the following claims. The culture at large is patriarchal. Patriarchy involves a division of labour between the male gazer and his female object. This division of labour affords pleasures that answer to psychological needs which drive the formation of gender identity in the first place. Pictures embody the male gaze and are designed to maximize its pleasures. The medium of depiction necessarily engages the male gaze in the sense that looking at any picture is like looking at a woman.

Autonomist feminist criticism

The orthodox account indicts not just some pictures of women, but most pictures of anything. As one commentator puts it, 'the feminist critique of representation rests on the equation: the medium = male = patriarchal = oppressive' (Devereaux 1995: 123). Furthermore, this equation, when conjoined with the claim that the male gaze aims to satisfy gendered, erotic pleasures, implies that these are the pleasures taken from most pictures. If taking these pleasures is immoral because it embodies or sustains patriarchal social structures, then looking at just about any picture is bad—though room must be made, somehow, for feminist art (Pollock 1991). This line of thought is at odds with the ambitions of this book: namely, to defend the aesthetic, cognitive, and moral merit of some pictures as vehicles for visual experience.

The view is not merely that women have been represented as objects of aesthetic delectation and that aesthetic evaluations have been used to sanitize dubious images. No doubt the dogma that erotic response is incompatible with aesthetic evaluation runs deep in our thinking. We have a tendency to deny that pictures with high aesthetic merit can possibly have prurient appeal. Provocations such as Charles Hope's calling Giorgione's and Titian's nudes 'mere pin-ups' (quoted in Freedberg 1989: 448) are useful if they compel us to confront what we are wont to overlook.

The orthodox account does not say that aesthetic evaluation is *misused* in covering up the erotic appeal of pictures. It holds considerably more strongly that the aesthetic appeal of pictures is an invention whose sole purpose is repression. As Anthea Callen writes, traditional art history and criticism 'construct a safe, aestheticizing language which mediates between the raw images and the consumer' (1991: 161). Findings of aesthetic merit license overlooking what is morally objectionable in pictures. They sugar a pill that activates attitudes oppressive to women. The antidote is to discount aesthetic considerations in favour of moral ones.

This stance assumes an autonomist conception of the relationship between moral and aesthetic evaluation. There is never any question that moral criticisms of pictures for pandering to the male gaze might imply aesthetic criticisms, and that those aesthetic criticisms might compete against purely formalist considerations that paper over the effects of the male gaze. Aesthetic evaluation is rehabilitated if it is made responsive to moral flaws.

Moralist feminist criticism

Autonomism was invented to protect aesthetic evaluation from what was quite rightly thought to be misplaced, prudish moral criticism. It has failed to achieve this aim: the segregation of aesthetic and moral evaluation has invited a wholesale rejection of the aesthetic. The best defence of aesthetic evaluation lies in moralism. The challenge is to show how to mount a robust feminist critique of the male gaze within a moralist framework.

The male gaze is discreditable because it is bound up with conceptions of gender that sustain patriarchal social structures. For the moralist, what is discreditable about the male gaze in pictures can be understood in terms of the moral sensibilities which the pictures project.

Feminist criticism within the image studies paradigm nicely fits the moral sensibilities approach. Posing, expression, viewpoint, spatial context, and medium may be handled so as to require the exercise of a concept of women as merely things to be looked at. Such a concept may figure in the content of emotional states, including those with erotic inflections. If the sight of female bodies depicted as merely to be looked at panders to sexual desire, and if sexual desire has as its intentional object visual experiences of female figures as things merely to be looked at, then the conceptual underpinnings of some pictures warrant moral condemnation.

Critics of the image studies approach complain that the male gaze is not confined to the nude and its direct offshoots (e.g. advertising images). For these critics, the orthodox account is superior because it takes the male gaze to be engaged in looking at any picture: it is the act of looking at the picture itself, not only a depicted female figure, that is gendered.

It is plausible that the male gaze roams beyond the nude, but it stretches the imagination that every picture—or every picture that is not self-consciously feminist—panders to the male gaze. Moralism suggests a compromise.

The male gaze may be engaged in looking at many kinds of pictures, not only those explicitly representing female bodies. The reason is that pictures help to shape their viewers' observational strategies. These observational strategies comprise two components: a disposition to discern certain features and a motivational component. The moralist may allow the male gaze to be engaged by any picture that requires and sustains observational patterns that are motivated by gendered sexual desire. If some pictures are apt merely to be ogled, and if there is a psychological connection between this ogling and the male gaze directed at the female body, then it is useful to think of the pictures as engaging the male gaze and so to condemn them. We may agree with critics of the image studies paradigm that the male gaze is not confined to the nude and its offshoots. It is not even confined to pictures of women. It becomes an empirical question how far, and in what directions, the male gaze roams in any culture at any historical moment.

The moralist proposal is neutral with regard to two tenets of the orthodox account. First, there is no commitment to the assumption that looking and all its pleasures *must* be gendered. Second, there is no commitment to a psychoanalytic explanation of the gendered origins of looking and the pleasure it yields. If looking need not be gendered, then there is no reason to seek a fact about human psychology that would explain why looking must be gendered. Neither tenet is required for a feminist criticism of the male gaze in many pictures, not just nudes.

Moral condemnation of the male gaze in a picture implies aesthetic condemnation when the picture's deployment of oppressive concepts is seen by a suitable observer (a feminist) to counteract the virtue of fine observation. Pictures pandering to the male gaze succeed only to the extent that their viewers are led to overlook important features of what they depict, to cling to familiar ways of seeing, and to be satisfied with initial visual impressions. Run-of-the-mill pornography and advertising are clear cases. This is not to deny that these images invite looking with concentration or a lingering eye—as David Freedberg remarks, 'there is a cognitive relation between...looking hard, not turning away, concentrating, and enjoying on one hand, and possession and arousal on the other' (1989: 325). Nevertheless, a motivated eye should be distinguished from a searching and reflective eye, and it is only the latter that is to be identified with fine observation and to be ruled out as incompatible with the male gaze.

Moral criticisms of pictures that pander to the male gaze may imply aesthetic criticisms. They may also foster a healthy scepticism about findings of aesthetic merit that function as a smoke-screen to obscure the work of the male gaze. Being pretty may be an aesthetic merit, as a rule, but it may be an aesthetic defect in a picture if it covers over other defects. There is something amiss with a picture that is pretty if it is otherwise heinous.

The moral failing of some pictures lies in the conception of gender that they embody and the kind of looking that this conception requires. To censure a picture that fails in this respect is to imply that it fails aesthetically. A vigorous feminist critique of the male gaze may be mounted within the framework of moralism.

Degas's nudes

Among those whose work has been investigated in the greatest detail and also stimulated the greatest debate among feminist critics and historians is Degas (Armstrong 1986; Kendall, Callen, and Gordon 1989; Kendall and Pollock 1991; Callen 1995). More than three-quarters of Degas's *œuvre* consists of pictures of women, from genre scenes and portraits to brothel scenes, laundresses, dancers, and nudes. Of these hundreds of images, the images of bathers,

Fig. 17. Edgar Degas, *The Tub (Bathing Woman)*, 1886. Photo credit: Erich Lessing/Art Resource, NY.

especially a series of six shown at the Impressionist Exhibition of 1886, have been taken as the key to Degas's work as a whole—an example is *The Tub*, reproduced in Figure 17.

In a ground-breaking work of feminist art history, Carol Armstrong places the bathers within the category of the nude, a genre 'with no other purpose but the deployment of the gaze and the brush—the "pure" acts of looking, forming, touching, painting, whose aim was to display as much while meaning as little as possible, to aestheticize and idealize the gaze and the object of delectation' (1986: 223). Many have stressed Degas's use of pastels to draw attention to facture and surface in these images, thereby aestheticizing them. The contorted poses of the figures and the unusually high or incoherent viewpoints from which they are depicted have the effect of disembodying the implied spectator. Thus Callen writes that Degas 'positioned his models expressly to avoid visual confrontation with the spectator. He reinforced the device of the averted eyes by exploiting poses which connote unselfconsciousness on the model's part' (1991: 165). She concludes that the images pander to the 'silent voyeuristic soliloquy' of the male gaze (1991: 166). Yet the image does not stop here, for 'the spectator...is made highly conscious of the act of spectating.... the subject of Degas's *Bathers* is indeed the voyeuristic gaze of the artist/spectator' (Callen 1995: 137). Armstrong, however, draws a different conclusion: Degas depicts

a female body that is entirely reflexive, existing in relation to itself, deflecting and excluding the viewer, refusing all exteriority. As such, it negates the traditional function of the female nude: to be present to the gaze of others; it negates as well the function of the nude's aestheticization and abstraction: to provide a sublimated mode of appropriation. (1986: 237)

Armstrong still finds that Degas's bathers embody notions of gender, but they are not modelled on the male gaze; rather, the represented figures possess interiority and physicality, in contrast to the absent male spectator whose traits are exteriority and disembodiment.

Although Armstrong's and Callen's conclusions are mutually inconsistent, they both not only condemn the pictures but credit them with drawing attention to and inviting reflection upon what is morally problematic in their depiction of women. Callen claims that the subject of the drawings is itself the male gaze, of which the spectator is made 'highly conscious'; while if Armstrong is correct, and the drawings repel the male gaze, replacing it with other gendered images of women, then they are bound to have a disturbing effect on viewers, whose expectations are frustrated.

Notice that the moral merit which Armstrong and Callen attribute to Degas's pastels is a step-up merit. Part of that merit depends on experiencing the pictures as disturbing the mechanism of the male gaze. It is only by seeing how the mechanism is disturbed that its grip on the viewer is loosened, so that he or she comes to see the male gaze at work in other images and in naked eye vision. The experience of the picture as disturbing is part of what makes being disturbing a merit in the picture. Evaluations of the picture as disturbing the male gaze are moral and also imply aesthetic evaluations.

As this case-study shows, feminist criticism of the male gaze can be nuanced and sophisticated. The nuances find better expression within a moralist framework than an autonomist one. Built into Armstrong's and Callen's accounts of Degas's 1886 pastels is a recognition that their moral flaws are ones on account of which the pictures are not wholly unredeemable—the pictures are redeemed in so far as they upset the workings of the male gaze. For the autonomist, the redemption is not aesthetic. For the moralist, by contrast, the redemption explains why the pictures have some aesthetic merit. It takes all the skills of fine observation to respond to the ways in which Degas upsets expectations.

Aesthetic evaluation is a deeply important element in human life, and the claim that it is in fact a mechanism for repression, directing us away from the true, sordid, nature of the pleasures we take in pictures, requires overwhelming arguments. An advantage of moralist criticism of the male gaze is that it does not require an error theory of the aesthetic. At the same time, it paves the way for a feminist critique of pictures to reclaim the aesthetic alongside the moral.

The original appeal of autonomism should be understood against the background of an overweening moralism that dominated art criticism until the beginning of the twentieth century and that made aesthetic merit contingent upon conformity to moral conventions. Autonomism liberated art criticism from its moral constraints, allowing for the recognition of aesthetic merits in morally flawed works. The irony is that autonomism also breeds the suspicion that when a work has aesthetic merits and serious moral flaws, the former function merely to cover up the latter. Interactionism shows the way out of the impasse. If some moral defects are aesthetic ones, or some aesthetic merits palliate moral defects, then moralist criticism has bite. At the same time, there is no question that the aesthetic is a sham to license indulging morally problematic thoughts or activities, for moral defects may be aesthetic defects.

AFTERWORD

Drawing isn't a matter of what you see; it's a question of what
you can make other people see.

Edgar Degas

It is no use promoting something to the status of art if that
means putting it forever on cognitive sabbatical.

Arthur Danto

The ambitions of this book have been to defend a robustly mimetic
conception of pictures and an interactionist view of their aesthetic
evaluation. The two aims nicely mesh if aesthetic evaluations of
pictures sometimes interact with cognitive ones and if cognition,
when it comes to pictures, is mimetic. The argument presented in
the previous five chapters rides this train of thought.

It thereby subverts a seeming dilemma that mars a great deal of
thinking about pictures: one might accept that pictures are mimetic
or that some aesthetic and cognitive evaluations interact, but one
cannot accept both.

The dilemma lies in the background of feminist criticism of the
male gaze in pictures. Pictures are proxies for the gaze because they
are mimetic; but since they also 'aestheticize' the gaze, we should
reject the aesthetic as a sham. The obvious response downplays the
mimetic dimension of pictures—it is formalist. Far less obvious is
the option of defending the aesthetic evaluation of pictures while
accepting their mimetic dimension.

One obstacle to seeing the appeal of interactionism is a conception
of cognitive evaluation that sidelines visual experience. It is hard to
see how measuring a picture's cognitive value can imply a finding of
aesthetic value as long as cognitive merit is thought to attach only to
such quantities as knowledge. In the extreme case, this obstacle

completely obscures the possibility that pictures, being mimetic, can make any real contribution to moral cognition.

The prospects for interactionism improve if aesthetic evaluations can take experiential form, and if visual experiences sometimes have cognitive merit in so far as they contribute to the development of visual sensibilities. The interactionist need only connect the two classes of experience.

Calvin Klein underwear ads do not teach us that women are merely things to be looked at, but they may teach us how to look at women as things to be looked at—they may change how we see things. If they do, that is a moral flaw in them. It is unlikely that Degas's bathers from 1886 teach us that women are *not* merely things to be looked at. What they may do is undermine habits of seeing women as eye candy, and if they do, then our experience of them as disturbing the gaze may be a moral and also an aesthetic evaluation. Is critical praise for *The Tub* (Fig. 17) as 'provocative' moral or aesthetic? Why not both?

The main obstacle to seeing the appeal of a mimetic conception of pictures is a narrow conception of seeing-in. The assumption is that to evaluate a picture as a picture is in part to evaluate it as a vehicle for experiences of seeing-in which resemble in important respects experiences of seeing what is depicted face to face. Given this assumption, how can seeing something in a picture differ in value from seeing the thing face to face in so far as they are alike?

The puzzle of mimesis depends on a virtual equation of seeing-in with seeing face to face. In fact, seeing something in a picture is always inflected by seeing the picture too. It is a mistake to infer that seeing-in is not seeing; the correct inference to draw is that seeing-in goes beyond seeing face to face. So long as seeing-in does not collapse into seeing face to face, evaluating a picture as a vehicle for seeing-in does not collapse into an evaluation of an experience of seeing face to face. Solving the puzzle of mimesis does not require denying that pictures are mimetic.

One might speculate as to whether the dilemma—choose between mimeticism and interactionism—underlies the recent turn in theoretical interest away from aesthetic evaluation to art evaluation.

After all, one way to solve the puzzle of mimesis not explored here is to evaluate pictures as art (Schier 1993). Granted that a picture of a pair of shoes affords the same kind of experience of shoes as seeing shoes face to face, the picture is nevertheless a product of human action in a way that seeing some shoes in the closet is not. Thus the value of the picture comes down to what is achieved in making it, given the career of its maker and the social setting in which it is made. The question then becomes whether cognitive and moral evaluations of pictures interact with evaluations of them as art— and this is a question which has recently received substantial attention (e.g. Jacobson 1997; Carroll 1996; Gaut 1998; Anderson and Dean 1998).

Although this solution to the puzzle of mimesis acknowledges the fact that pictures are mimetic devices, it also turns its back on that fact's evaluative relevance. That is, it declines to dispute the idea that there is no difference in value between seeing shoes in a van Gogh painting and seeing shoes in a closet in so far as both are seeing shoes. Of course, some pictures are rightly evaluated as art, and there are many worthwhile theoretical questions that art evaluation raises. Turning to these questions changes the topic from the evaluation of pictures as vehicles for seeing-in.

The seeming dilemma that mars thinking about pictures is that we must choose between accepting that pictures are mimetic and accepting that aesthetic, cognitive, and moral evaluations of pictures sometimes interact. The dilemma is a false one: it is possible to accept mimeticism and interactionism, given the right conception of what each involves.

This does not go far enough. Accepting interactionism is made much easier by accepting that pictures are robustly visual because they sustain seeing-in. An aesthetic evaluation of a picture as a picture is an evaluation of it that is, or is tied to, an experience of seeing-in. According to interactionism, some aesthetic evaluations imply or are implied by cognitive evaluations of pictures. The crux is the cognitive value of seeing-in. We would not be the aesthetic appreciators that we are were we unable to see things in pictures. Would we be the thinkers, knowers, and understanders that we are without the ability to see things in pictures and to evaluate them accordingly? A virtue of the argument in this book is its answering 'no'.

Perhaps, to adapt David Lewis, the purpose of arguments in philosophy is to measure the price of our commitments. The price you pay if you accept the argument in this book is that the contents of visual experience are very rich. They include seeing scenes in pictures, seeing expressions in pictures, and seeing pictures as strengthening or weakening the quality of seeing itself. None of this is seeing with an innocent eye—it is informed by non-visual thought—and that discounts the price. Nevertheless, it is clear that we need a theory of the contents of visual experience. Unless visual experience can have rich contents, we must return to the drawing-board. This is no reason to fret. Vermeer's woman holding a balance knows that a high price can be good value: we make progress when we substitute one problem for another.

REFERENCES

Alberti, Leon Battista (1966) *On Painting*, trans. John R. Spencer. New Haven: Yale University Press.

Anderson, James, and Jeffrey Dean (1998) 'Moderate Autonomism'. *British Journal of Aesthetics* 38: 150–66.

Aristotle (1987) *The Poetics of Aristotle*, trans. Stephen Halliwell. Chapel Hill, NC: University of North Carolina Press.

Armstrong, Carol M. (1986) 'Edgar Degas and the Representation of the Female Body'. In *The Female Body in Western Culture*, ed. Susan Rubin Suleiman. Cambridge, Mass.: Harvard University Press.

Baxandall, Michael (1985) *Patterns of Intention*. New Haven: Yale University Press.

—— (1988) *Painting and Experience in Fifteenth Century Italy*. Oxford: Oxford University Press.

Beardsley, Monroe C. (1979) 'In Defense of Aesthetic Value'. *Proceedings of the American Philosophical Association* 52: 723–49.

—— (1981) *Aesthetics*, 2nd edn. Indianapolis: Hackett.

Bell, Clive (1913) *Art*. London: Chatto and Windus.

Bell, Julian (1999) *What Is Painting?* London: Thames and Hudson.

Bender, John W. (1996) 'Realism, Supervenience, and Irresolvable Aesthetic Disputes'. *Journal of Aesthetics and Art Criticism* 54: 371–81.

Berger, John (1972) *Ways of Seeing*. Harmondsworth: Penguin.

Bermudez, Jose Luis, and Sebastian Gardner, eds. (2003) *Art and Morality*. London: Routledge.

Booth, Wayne C. (1988) *The Company We Keep: An Ethics of Fiction*. Berkeley: University of California Press.

Boyd, Patrick (1993) *Perception and Passion in Dante's Comedy*. Cambridge: Cambridge University Press.

Budd, Malcolm (1993) 'How Pictures Look'. In *Virtue and Taste*, ed. Dudley Knowles and John Skorupski. Oxford: Blackwell.

—— (1995) *Values of Art: Pictures, Poetry, and Music*. Harmondsworth: Penguin.

Callen, Anthea (1991) 'Degas' *Bathers:* Hygene and Dirt, Gaze and Touch'. In *Dealing with Degas*, ed. Richard Kendall and Griselda Pollock. New York: Universe.

—— (1995) *The Spectacular Body.* New Haven: Yale University Press.

Carroll, Noël (1985) 'The Specificity of Media in the Arts'. *Journal of Aesthetic Education* 19: 5–20.

—— (1995) 'The Image of Women in Film'. In *Feminism and Tradition in Aesthetics*, ed. Peggy Zeglin Brand and Carolyn Korsmeyer. University Park, Pa.: Pennsylvania State University Press.

—— (1996) 'Moderate Moralism'. *British Journal of Aesthetics* 36: 223–37.

—— (1998) *A Philosophy of Mass Art.* Oxford: Oxford University Press.

—— (2000) 'Art and Ethical Criticism'. *Ethics* 110: 350–87.

Code, Lorraine (1987) *Epistemic Responsibility.* Hanover, NH: University Press of New England.

Cohen, Jonathan, and Aaron Meskin (2004) 'On the Epistemic Value of Photographs'. *Journal of Aesthetics and Art Criticism* 62: 197–210.

Crow, Thomas (1999) *The Intelligence of Art.* Chapel Hill, NC: University of North Carolina Press.

Currie, Gregory (1997) 'The Moral Psychology of Fiction'. In *Art and Its Messages*, ed. Stephen Davies. University Park, Pa.: Pennsylvania State University Press.

—— (1998) 'Realism of Character and the Value of Fiction'. In *Aesthetics and Ethics: Essays at the Intersection*, ed. Jerrold Levinson. Cambridge: Cambridge University Press.

Dante (1985*a*) *Dante's Inferno*, trans. and illus. Tom Phillips. London and New York: Thames and Hudson.

—— (1985*b*) *Purgatorio*, trans. Mark Musa. Harmondsworth: Penguin.

—— (1994) *The Inferno of Dante*, trans. Robert Pinsky. New York: Farrar, Straus, Giroux.

Danto, Arthur C. (1996) *Playing with the Edge: The Photographic Achievement of Robert Mapplethorpe.* Berkeley: University of California Press.

Davies, David (2004) *Art as Performance.* Oxford: Blackwell.

Davies, Stephen (1980) 'The Expression of Emotion in Music'. *Mind* 89: 67–86.

—— ed. (1997) *Art and Its Messages.* University Park, Pa.: Pennsylvania State University Press.

Devereaux, Mary (1995) 'Oppressive Texts, Resisting Readers, and the Gendered Spectator'. In *Feminism and Tradition in Aesthetics*, ed. Peggy

Zeglin Brand and Carolyn Korsmeyer. University Park, Pa.: Pennsylvania State University Press.

Dickie, George (1988) *Evaluating Art*. Philadelphia: Temple University Press.

Dretske, Fred (1981) *Knowledge and the Flow of Information*. Oxford: Blackwell.

——(1988) *Explaining Behavior: Reasons in a World of Causes*. Cambridge, Mass: MIT Press.

Eaton, Marcia (1980) 'Truth in Pictures'. *Journal of Aesthetics and Art Criticism* 39: 15–26.

——(1994) 'The Intrinsic, Non-Supervenient Nature of Aesthetic Properties'. *Journal of Aesthetics and Art Criticism* 52: 383–97.

Ekman, Paul (1980) 'Biological and Cultural Contributions to Body and Facial Movement in the Expression of Emotions'. In *Explaining Emotions*, ed. Amelie Rorty. Berkeley: University of California Press.

——(1984) 'Expression and the Nature of Emotion'. In *Approaches to Emotion*, ed. Klaus Scherer and Paul Ekman. Hillsdale, NJ: Lawrence Erlbaum.

—— Wallace V. Friesen, and Phoebe Ellsworth (1982) 'What are the Relative Contributions of Facial Behavior and Contextual Information to the Judgement of Emotion?' In *Emotion in the Human Face*, ed. Paul Ekman. Cambridge: Cambridge University Press.

Feagin, Susan (1995) 'Paintings and their Places'. In *Art and Its Messages*, ed. Stephen Davies. University Park, Pa.: Pennsylvania State University Press.

——(1998) 'Presentation and Representation'. *Journal of Aesthetics and Art Criticism* 56: 234–40.

Fodor, Jerry (1990) *A Theory of Content and Other Essays*. Cambridge, Mass.: MIT Press.

Forceville, Charles (2004) 'Visual Representations of the Idealized Cognitive Model of Anger in the Asterix Album La Zizanie'. *Journal of Pragmatics* 36: 69–88.

Freedberg, David (1989) *The Power of Images*. Chicago: University of Chicago Press.

Fry, Roger (1927) 'Some Questions in Esthetics'. In *Transformations*. London: Chatto and Windus.

——(1992) 'An Essay in Aesthetics'. In *Art in Theory 1900–1990*, ed. Andrew Harrison and Paul Wood. Oxford: Blackwell.

Gage, John (1993) *Color and Culture*. Boston: Little, Brown.

Gaut, Berys (1998) 'The Ethical Criticism of Art'. In *Aesthetics and Ethics: Essays at the Intersection*, ed. Jerrold Levinson. Cambridge: Cambridge University Press.

Gibbard, Alan (1992) 'Morality and Thick Concepts'. *Proceedings of the Aristotelian Society* 66: 267–83.

Gibson, James J. (1979) *The Ecological Approach to Visual Perception*. Boston: Houghton Mifflin.

Goldman, Alan (1995*a*) *Aesthetic Value*. Boulder, Colo.: Westview Press.

—— (1995*b*) 'The Aesthetic Value of Representation in Painting'. *Philosophy and Phenomenological Research* 55: 297–310.

Gombrich, E. H. (1961) *Art and Illusion*. Princeton: Princeton University Press.

—— (1973) 'Illusion and Art'. In *Illusion in Nature and Art*, ed. Richard Gregory and E. H. Gombrich. London: Duckworth.

—— (1978) 'Expression and Communication'. In *Meditations on a Hobby Horse*. Oxford: Phaidon.

—— (1982*a*) 'Ritualized Gesture and Expression in Art'. In *The Image and the Eye*. Oxford: Phaidon.

—— (1982*b*) 'Visual Discovery through Art'. In *The Image and the Eye*. Oxford: Phaidon.

Goodman, Nelson (1976) *Languages of Art*, 2nd edn. Indianapolis: Hackett.

Graham, Gordon (1994) 'Value and the Visual Arts'. *Journal of Aesthetic Education* 28: 1–14.

—— (1995) 'Learning from Art'. *British Journal of Aesthetics* 35: 26–37.

Greenberg, Clement (1961) *Art and Culture*. Boston: Beacon.

Grice, H. P. (1975) 'Logic and Conversation'. In *The Logic of Grammar*, ed. Donald Davidson and Gilbert Harman. Encino, Calif.: Dickenson.

Guyer, Paul (1998) 'Baumgarten'. In *Encyclopedia of Aesthetics*, ed. Michael Kelly. Oxford: Oxford University Press.

Hampshire, Stuart (1959) 'Logic and Appreciation'. In *Aesthetics and Language*, ed. William Elton. Oxford: Blackwell.

Harrison, Andrew (1973) 'Representation and Conceptual Change'. In *Philosophy and the Arts*. London: Macmillan.

Haskell, Francis (1993) *History and Its Images: Art and the Interpretation of the Past*. New Haven: Yale University Press.

Hookway, Christopher (1994) 'Cognitive Virtues and Epistemic Evaluations'. *International Journal of Philosophical Studies* 2: 211–27.

Hopkins, Robert (1997) 'Pictures and Beauty'. *Proceedings of the Aristotelian Society* 42: 177–94.

—— (1998) *Picture, Image, and Experience*. Cambridge: Cambridge University Press.

—— (2000) 'Touching Pictures'. *British Journal of Aesthetics* 40: 149–67.

—— (2005) 'What Is Pictorial Representation?' In *Contemporary Debates in the Philosophy of Art*, ed. Matthew Kieran. Oxford: Blackwell.

Hospers, John (1946) *Meaning and Truth in the Arts*. Chapel Hill, NC: University of North Carolina Press.

Hume, David (1777) *Enquiries*. London: Cadell.

Hursthouse, Rosalind (1992) 'Truth and Representation'. In *Philosophical Aesthetics*, ed. Oswald Hanfling. Oxford: Blackwell.

Hutcheson, Francis (1973) *An Inquiry Concerning Beauty, Order, Harmony, and Design*, ed. Peter Kivy. The Hague: Martinus Nijhoff.

Hyman, John (2000) 'Pictorial Art and Visual Experience'. *British Journal of Aesthetics* 40: 21–45.

Iseminger, Gary (1981) 'Aesthetic Appreciation'. *Journal of Aesthetics and Art Criticism* 39: 389–97.

Isenberg, Arnold (1949) 'Critical Communication'. *Philosophical Review* 58: 330–44.

Ivins, William J., Jr. (1962) *Art and Geometry: A Study in Space Intuitions*. New York: Dover.

Jacobson, Daniel (1997) 'In Praise of Immoral Art'. *Philosophical Topics* 25: 155–200.

Jameson, Fredric (1990) *Signatures of the Visible*. New York: Routledge.

John, Eileen (1998) 'Reading Fiction and Conceptual Knowledge'. *Journal of Aesthetics and Art Criticism* 56: 331–48.

Kant, Immanuel (1987) *Critique of Judgement*, trans. Werner Pluhar. Indianapolis: Hackett.

Kaplan, E. Ann (1983) 'Is the Gaze Male?' In *Powers of Desire*, ed. Ann Snitow, Christine Stansell, and Sharon Thompson. New York: Monthly Review Press.

Kendall, Richard, Anthea Callen, and Dillian Gordon (1989) *Degas: Images of Women*. Liverpool: Tate Gallery.

—— and Griselda Pollock, eds. (1991) *Dealing with Degas*. New York: Universe.

Kennedy, John M. (1993) *Drawing and the Blind: Pictures to Touch*. New Haven: Yale University Press.

Kieran, Matthew (1996) 'Art, Imagination, and the Cultivation of Morals'. *Journal of Aesthetics and Art Criticism* 54: 337–51.

Kirkpatrick, Robin (1987) *Dante: The Divine Comedy*. Cambridge: Cambridge University Press.

Kivy, Peter (1989) *Sound Sentiment*. Philadelphia: Temple University Press.

Kornblith, Hilary (1983) 'Justified Belief and Epistemically Responsible Action'. *Philosophical Review* 92: 33–48.

Korsmeyer, Carolyn (1985) 'Pictorial Assertion'. *Journal of Aesthetics and Art Criticism* 43: 257–65.

Kulvicki, John (2003) 'Image Structure'. *Journal of Aesthetics and Art Criticism* 61: 323–40.

Lamarque, Peter, and Stein Haugom Olsen (1994) *Truth, Fiction, and Literature*. Oxford: Oxford University Press.

Le Brun, Charles (2000) 'Conference on Expression'. In *Art in Theory: 1648–1815*, ed. Charles Harrison, Paul Wood, and Jason Gaiger. Oxford: Blackwell.

Lebrun, Rico (1968) *Drawings*. Berkeley: University of California Press.

Lessing, Gotthold (1962) *Laocoon*, trans. E. A. McCormick. Indianapolis: Bobbs-Merrill.

Levinson, Jerrold (1990) 'Artworks and the Future'. In *Music, Art, and Metaphysics*. Ithaca, NY: Cornell University Press.

——(1994) 'Being Realistic about Aesthetic Properties'. *Journal of Aesthetics and Art Criticism* 52: 351–4.

——(1996*a*) 'Musical Expressiveness'. In *The Pleasures of Aesthetics*. Ithaca, NY: Cornell University Press.

——(1996*b*) 'Pleasure and the Value of Works of Art'. In *The Pleasures of Aesthetics*. Ithaca, NY: Cornell University Press.

——ed. (1998) *Aesthetics and Ethics: Essays at the Intersection*. Cambridge: Cambridge University Press.

Lippard, Lucy (1992) 'Andres Serrano: The Spirit and the Letter'. In *Culture Wars: Documents from Recent Controversies in the Arts*, ed. Richard Bolton. New York: New Press.

Lopes, Dominic McIver (1996) *Understanding Pictures*. Oxford: Oxford University Press.

——(1997) 'Art Media and the Sense Modalities: Tactile Pictures'. *Philosophical Quarterly* 47: 425–40.

——(2002) 'Vision, Touch, and the Value of Pictures'. *British Journal of Aesthetics* 42: 191–201.

——(2003*a*) 'Out of Sight, Out of Mind'. In *Philosophy, Imagination, and the Arts*, ed. Matthew Kieran and Dominic McIver Lopes. London: Routledge.

—— (2003*b*) 'Pictures and the Representational Mind'. *Monist* 86: 32–52.

Matisse, Henri (1992) 'Notes of a Painter'. In *Art in Theory: 1900–1990*, ed. Charles Harrison and Paul Wood. Oxford: Blackwell.

Matravers, Derek (1998) *Art and Emotion*. Oxford: Oxford University Press.

Minio-Paluello, Lorenzo (1980) 'Dante's Reading of Aristotle'. In *The World of Dante*, ed. Cecil Grayson. Oxford: Oxford University Press.

Mitchell, W. J. T. (1986) *Iconology: Image, Text, Ideology*. Chicago: University of Chicago Press.

Montagu, Jennifer (1994) *The Expression of the Passions*. New Haven: Yale University Press.

Morgan, Douglas N. (1953) 'On Pictorial Truth'. *Philosophical Studies* 4: 17–23.

Mothersill, Mary (1984) *Beauty Restored*. Oxford: Oxford University Press.

Mulvey, Laura (1989) 'Visual Pleasure and Narrative Cinema'. In *Visual Pleasure and Other Pleasures*. Bloomington, Ind.: Indiana University Press.

Nassar, Eugene Paul (1994) *Illustrations to Dante's Inferno*. Cranbury, NJ: Associated University Presses.

Newall, Michael (2003) 'A Restriction for Pictures and Some Consequences for a Theory of Depiction'. *Journal of Aesthetics and Art Criticism* 61: 381–94.

Novitz, David (1977) *Pictures and Their Use in Communication*. The Hague: Martinus Nijhoff.

—— (1987) *Knowledge, Fiction, and Imagination*. Philadelphia: Temple University Press.

Nussbaum, Martha (1990) *Love's Knowledge*. Oxford: Oxford University Press.

Peacocke, Christopher (1987) 'Depiction'. *Philosophical Review* 96: 383–410.

Peirce, C. S. (1931) *Collected Papers of Charles Sanders Peirce*. Cambridge, Mass.: Harvard University Press.

Pettit, Philip (1983) 'Aesthetic Realism'. In *Pleasure, Preference, and Value*, ed. Eva Schaper. Cambridge: Cambridge University Press.

Podro, Michael (1998) *Depiction*. New Haven: Yale University Press.

Pollock, Griselda (1988) *Vision and Difference: Femininity, Feminism and Histories of Art*. London: Routledge.

—— (1991) 'The Gaze and the Look: Women with Binoculars'. In *Dealing with Degas*, ed. Richard Kendall and Griselda Pollock. New York: Universe.

Poussin, Nicholas (1958) 'Letter to Chantelou of November 24, 1647'. In *A Documentary History of Art*, ed. Elizabeth Gilmore Holt. New York: Doubleday.

Reid, Louis Arnaud (1980) 'Art: Knowing-That and Knowing-This'. *British Journal of Aesthetics* 20: 329–39.

Robinson, Jenefer (1994) 'The Expression and Arousal of Emotion in Music'. *Journal of Aesthetics and Art Criticism* 52: 13–22.

—— (2005) *Deeper than Reason: Emotion and its Role in Literature, Music, and Art*. Oxford: Oxford University Press.

Roskill, Mark, and David Carrier (1983) *Truth and Falsehood in Visual Images*. Amherst, Mass.: University of Massachusetts Press.

Ross, Stephanie (1984) 'Painting the Passions: Charles Lebrun's *Conference sur l'Expression*'. *Journal of the History of Ideas* 45: 25–47.

Savile, Anthony (1986) 'Imagination and Pictorial Understanding'. *Aristotelian Society Supplementary Volume* 60: 19–44.

—— (1987) *Aesthetic Reconstructions*. Oxford: Blackwell.

Scheffler, Israel (1991) 'In Praise of the Cognitive Emotions'. In *In Praise of the Cognitive Emotions*. New York: Routledge.

Schier, Flint (1986) *Deeper Into Pictures*. Cambridge: Cambridge University Press.

—— (1993) 'Van Gogh's Boots: The Claims of Representation'. In *Virtue and Taste*, ed. Dudley Knowles and John Skorupski. Oxford: Blackwell.

Schwartz, Robert (1985) 'The Power of Pictures'. *Journal of Philosophy* 82: 711–20.

Sharpe, R. A. (2000) 'The Empiricist Theory of Artistic Value'. *Journal of Aesthetics and Art Criticism* 58: 321–32.

Shelley, James (2004) 'The Experience Theory of Aesthetic Value'. Paper presented at the American Society for Aesthetics Annual Meeting, Houston, 28 October 2004.

Sibley, Frank (2001*a*) 'Aesthetic Concepts'. In *Approach to Aesthetics*, ed. John Benson, Betty Redfern, and Jeremy Roxbee Cox. Oxford: Oxford University Press.

—— (2001*b*) 'Aesthetic, Non-Aesthetic'. In *Approach to Aesthetics*.

—— (2001*c*) 'Originality and Value'. In *Approach to Aesthetics*.

Smith, Barbara Herrnstein (1988) *Contingencies of Value*. Cambridge, Mass.: Harvard University Press.

Sontag, Susan (1979) *On Photography*. Harmondsworth: Penguin.

Sosa, Ernest (1991) *Knowledge in Perspective*. Cambridge: Cambridge University Press.

Stafford, Barbara (1996) *Good Looking: Essays on the Virtues of Images*. Cambridge, Mass.: MIT Press.

Stecker, Robert (1997) *Artworks: Definition, Meaning, Value*. University Park, Pa.: Pennsylvania State University Press.

—— (2005) *Aesthetics and the Philosophy of Art: An Introduction*. Lanham, Md.: Rowman and Littlefield.

Stolnitz, Jerome (1992) 'On the Cognitive Triviality of Art'. *British Journal of Aesthetics* 32: 191–200.

Strawson, P. F. (1974) 'Aesthetic Appraisal and Works of Art'. In *Freedom and Resentment*. London: Methuen.

Stump, Eleonore (1986) 'Dante's Hell, Aquinas's Moral Theory, and the Love of God'. *Canadian Journal of Philosophy* 16: 181–98.

Testelin, Henri (2000) 'Table of Precepts: Expression'. In *Art in Theory: 1648–1815*, ed. Charles Harrison, Paul Wood, and Jason Gaiger. Oxford: Blackwell.

Tilghman, Ben (1996) 'A Conceptual Dimension of Art History'. In *Gombrich on Art and Psychology*, ed. Richard Woodfield. Manchester: Manchester University Press.

Urmson, J. O. (1957) 'What Makes a Situation Aesthetic?' *Proceedings of the Aristotelian Society* 31: 75–92.

Vermazen, Bruce (1975) 'Comparing Evaluations of Works of Art'. *Journal of Aesthetics and Art Criticism* 34: 7–14.

—— (1986) 'Expression as Expression'. *Pacific Philosophical Quarterly* 67: 196–234.

—— (1988) 'Aesthetic Satisfaction'. In *Human Agency: Language, Duty, and Value*, ed. C. C. W. Taylor. Stanford, Calif.: Stanford University Press.

—— (1991) 'The Aesthetic Value of Originality'. *Midwest Studies in Philosophy* 16: 266–79.

Vinci, Leonardo da (1989) *Leonardo on Painting*, trans. Martin Kemp. New Haven: Yale University Press.

Walsh, Dorothy (1969) *Literature and Knowledge*. Middletown, Conn.: Wesleyan University Press.

Walton, Kendall (1970) 'Categories of Art'. *Philosophical Review* 79: 334–67.

—— (1990) *Mimesis as Make-Believe*. Cambridge, Mass.: Harvard University Press.

Weyergraf-Serra, Clara, and Martha Buskirk, eds. (1988) *Richard Serra's Tilted Arc.* Eindhoven: Van Abbemuseum.

Williams, Bernard (1985) *Ethics and the Limits of Philosophy.* Cambridge, Mass.: Harvard University Press.

Wilson, Catherine (1983) 'Literature and Knowledge'. *Philosophy* 58: 489–96.

Wittgenstein, Ludwig (1953) *Philosophical Investigations*, trans. G. E. M. Anscombe. Oxford: Blackwell.

—— (1967) *Lectures and Conversations on Aesthetics, Psychology, and Religious Belief.* Berkeley: University of California Press.

Wollheim, Richard (1980) 'Seeing-as, Seeing-in, and Pictorial Representation'. In *Art and its Objects.* Cambridge: Cambridge University Press.

—— (1987) *Painting as an Art.* London and New York: Thames and Hudson.

—— (1993) 'Correspondence, Projective Properties, and Expression in the Arts'. In *The Mind and Its Depths.* Cambridge, Mass.: Harvard University Press.

—— (1998) 'Pictorial Representation'. *Journal of Aesthetics and Art Criticism* 56: 217–26.

Young, James O. (1995) 'Evaluation and the Cognitive Function of Art'. *Journal of Aesthetic Education* 29: 65–78.

—— (1996) 'Inquiry in the Arts and Sciences'. *Philosophy* 71: 255–73.

Zagzebski, Linda Trinkaus (1996) *Virtues of the Mind.* Cambridge: Cambridge University Press.

Zangwill, Nick (2001) *The Metaphysics of Beauty.* Ithaca, NY: Cornell University Press.

Ziff, Paul (1958) 'Reasons in Art Criticism'. In *Philosophy and Education*, ed. Israel Scheffler. Boston: Allyn and Bacon.

INDEX